MW00953232

Power BI DAX Dictionary

Function-by-Function Explained

Table of Contents

Introduction

Welcome everyone to the book **"Power BI DAX Dictionary: Function-by-Function Explained"** In today's era of digital transformation, the power of data cannot be underestimated. Power BI, one of the renowned tools for Business Intelligence and data analysis, has become a crucial instrument in transforming data into valuable insights and gaining a deeper understanding of business.

Power BI is a dynamic suite of business analytics tools developed by Microsoft, designed to empower organizations with interactive visualizations and business intelligence capabilities. It allows users to connect to various data sources, transform raw data into meaningful information, and share insights across the organization.

DAX (Data Analysis Expressions), on the other hand, is the formula language used in Power BI and other Microsoft tools like Excel Power Pivot and Analysis Services Tabular. DAX is the key to unlocking the full potential of Power BI, enabling users to create sophisticated calculations and custom measures to analyze data in powerful ways.

In **"Power BI DAX Dictionary: Function-by-Function Explained"** we embark on a comprehensive journey through the world of DAX functions. DAX can be a formidable landscape to navigate, but fear not! This book is your guide, breaking down each function, explaining its purpose, syntax, and usage, and providing practical examples to illustrate how it can be applied in real-world scenarios.

Whether you are a data analyst, business intelligence professional, or simply someone interested in harnessing the power of data for better decision-making, this book is designed to be your companion in mastering DAX functions within the context of Power BI.

In each chapter, we will explore a specific group of DAX functions, categorizing them based on their functional purposes, demystifying their complexities, and equipping you with the tools to effectively harness their potential. By the conclusion of this book, you will possess a strong grasp of these DAX function groups and the confidence to apply them for extracting actionable insights from your data.

Get ready to explore the Function-by-Function DAX Dictionary, and let's embark on a journey of data discovery and analytical excellence with Power BI!

CHAPTER I
Chart Functions

1. COUNTROWS

Syntax:

COUNTROWS(table)

- `table`: This is the table or table expression you want to count the number of rows from.

Description:

The COUNTROWS function in Power BI DAX is used to count the number of rows (records) in a table or table expression. This function is commonly used for data analysis and creating statistical charts based on the count of rows that meet specific conditions.

Example:

Suppose you have a "Sales" table containing information about sales transactions, and you want to know how many transactions are in this table.

DAX Formula:

Total Sales = COUNTROWS(Sales)

Result: If the "Sales" table contains 1000 transaction records, the formula will return the value 1000.

Tips:

- **COUNTROWS** is particularly useful when you want to count the number of rows that meet specific conditions. You can combine it with other DAX functions like **FILTER** to count rows based on criteria.

Example:

You want to count the number of transactions in the "Sales" table with amounts greater than $1000:

High Value Sales = COUNTROWS(FILTER(Sales, Sales[Amount] > 1000))

This formula will return the count of transactions that meet the condition of having an amount greater than $1000.

- When using COUNTROWS, ensure that the argument provided is a valid table or table expression. It's essential to understand the structure of your data model and the tables you're working with.

Note: The examples provided here assume a simplified data model and dataset for illustration purposes. In a real-world scenario, the data model and dataset may be more complex.

2. CROSSJOIN

Syntax:

CROSSJOIN(table1, table2)

- `table1`: The first table or table expression to be joined.

- `table2`: The second table or table expression to be joined.

Description:

The **CROSSJOIN** function in Power BI DAX is used to create a new table by combining all possible combinations of rows from two tables. It generates a Cartesian product of the rows from both tables, resulting in a larger table.

Example:

Let's say you have two tables: "Products" and "Colors," and you want to create a table that lists all possible combinations of products and colors.

DAX Formula:

ProductColorCombinations = CROSSJOIN(Products, Colors)

Result: The "ProductColorCombinations" table will contain all possible combinations of products and colors. If "Products" has 10 rows and "Colors" has 5 rows, the result will be a table with 10 * 5 = 50 rows, representing every possible product-color combination.

Tips:

- Use **CROSSJOIN** carefully, as it can lead to the creation of large tables with many rows. It's often used when you need to perform calculations involving all possible combinations, such as calculating sales for every product-color combination.

Example:

Suppose you have a "Sales" table with transactions, and you want to analyze sales by product-color combination. You can create a "ProductColorCombinations" table using **CROSSJOIN** and then use it to calculate sales.

ProductColorCombinations = CROSSJOIN(Products, Colors)

SalesByProductColor = SUMX(ProductColorCombinations, CALCULATE(SUM(Sales[Amount])))

This allows you to analyze sales for each product-color combination.

- Be mindful of performance when using **CROSSJOIN** with large tables. It can lead to slower query performance and increased memory usage. Consider filtering or reducing the size of the tables before applying **CROSSJOIN** if necessary.

Note: The examples provided here assume a simplified data model and dataset for illustration purposes. In a real-world scenario, the data model and dataset may be more complex.

3. NATURALLEFTOUTERJOIN

Syntax:

NATURALLEFTOUTERJOIN(table1, table2)

- `table1`: The first table or table expression.

- `table2`: The second table or table expression.

Description:

The **NATURALLEFTOUTERJOIN** function in Power BI DAX is used to perform a natural left outer join operation between two tables. This function combines rows from both tables where the values in the common columns match, and it includes all rows from the left table (table1) and only the matching rows from the right table (table2). If there are no matches, the result will still contain all rows from the left table with null values for columns from the right table.

Example:

Suppose you have two tables: "Employees" and "Departments." The "Employees" table contains employee information, including a "DepartmentID" column, and the "Departments" table contains department details, including a "DepartmentID" column. You want to perform a natural left outer join to combine these tables based on the common "DepartmentID" column.

DAX Formula:

EmployeeDepartmentInfo = NATURALLEFTOUTERJOIN(Employees, Departments)

Result: The "EmployeeDepartmentInfo" table will contain all employee records along with their respective department details. If an employee does not belong to any department, the corresponding department columns will have null values.

Tips:

- Use **NATURALLEFTOUTERJOIN** when you need to combine tables based on common columns, and you want to retain all rows from the left table while including matching rows from the right table.

- Be cautious when dealing with large datasets, as left outer joins can result in a significant number of rows. Consider filtering or reducing the dataset size before applying the join if necessary.

- Ensure that the common columns used for joining have the same names and data types in both tables for the natural join to work effectively.

The **NATURALLEFTOUTERJOIN** function simplifies the process of merging data from two tables, especially when they have common columns, making it a valuable tool for data modeling and analysis in Power BI.

4. RELATED

Syntax:

RELATED(table_name[column_name])

- `table_name`: The name of the related table.

- `column_name`: The name of the column from the related table whose value you want to retrieve.

Description:

The RELATED function in Power BI DAX is a powerful tool for retrieving values from a related table. It is used in scenarios where there is an established relationship between tables, and you need to fetch data from a related (connected) table based on that relationship.

Example:

Suppose you have two tables: "Sales" and "Products." The "Sales" table contains information about sales transactions, including a "ProductID" column, and the "Products" table contains details about various products, including the same "ProductID" column. To retrieve the product name associated with each sale in the "Sales" table, you can use the RELATED function.

DAX Formula:

Sales[ProductName] = RELATED(Products[ProductName])

Result: The "Sales" table will now include a "ProductName" column, and for each sale, it will display the corresponding product name from the "Products" table based on the matching "ProductID."

Tips:

- Ensure that there is an established relationship between the tables for the RELATED function to work correctly. You can create relationships using Power BI's relationship editor.

- Use **RELATED** when you need to fetch data from a related table within calculated columns or measures. It simplifies the process of data retrieval without the need for complex joins or lookups.

- Be cautious with performance when using **RELATED,** especially with large datasets. Fetching data from related tables can have performance implications, so optimize your data model and relationships as needed.

The **RELATED** function is a fundamental feature of Power BI's modeling capabilities, enabling you to create more insightful reports and dashboards by seamlessly connecting data across tables.

5. RELATEDTABLE

Syntax:

RELATEDTABLE(table_name)

- `table_name`: The name of the related table for which you want to retrieve the table or table expression.

Description:

The **RELATEDTABLE** function in Power BI DAX is used to retrieve a table or table expression related to the current row from another table based on an established relationship. This function is valuable when you need to access related data for calculations or filtering within measures and calculated columns.

Example:

Imagine you have two tables: "Orders" and "Products." The "Orders" table contains order details with a "ProductID" column, and the "Products" table includes information about various products, including a "ProductID" column. To retrieve a table of products related to each order in the "Orders" table, you can utilize the RELATEDTABLE function.

DAX Formula:

RelatedProducts = RELATEDTABLE(Products)

Result: The "RelatedProducts" table will contain all the product details associated with each order. It effectively filters the "Products" table to include only the relevant products for each order based on the established relationship.

Tips:

- Ensure that there is an established relationship between the tables for the **RELATEDTABLE** function to function correctly. You can create relationships using Power BI's relationship editor.

- Use **RELATEDTABLE** when you need to retrieve related data in a tabular format for further analysis or calculations within your measures or calculated columns.

- Be mindful of the potential size of the resulting table when using **RELATEDTABLE,** especially with large datasets. It can affect performance and memory usage, so optimize your data model accordingly.

The **RELATEDTABLE** function is a valuable tool for accessing related data tables, simplifying the process of data extraction and analysis in Power BI's modeling and reporting capabilities.

6. TREATAS

Syntax:

TREATAS(expression, table[column])

- `expression`: The expression or values you want to treat as if they are part of the specified column.

- `table[column]`: The column within a table whose values you want to treat as the filter context.

Description:

The **TREATAS** function in Power BI DAX is used to temporarily replace the filter context of one column with the filter context of another column. It's particularly useful when you want to apply filters from one table to another related table or when you need to override the default filter context for a specific calculation.

Example:

Suppose you have two tables: "Sales" and "Calendar." The "Sales" table contains sales transactions with a "DateID" column, and the "Calendar" table includes a "Date" column. To calculate total sales for a specific date range defined in the "Calendar" table, you can use the **TREATAS** function.

DAX Formula:

TotalSalesInRange =

```
SUMX(

    FILTER(

        Sales,

        TREATAS(

            VALUES(Calendar[Date]),

            Sales[DateID]

        )

    ),

    Sales[Amount]

)
```

Result: The "TotalSalesInRange" measure will sum the "Amount" column from the "Sales" table for the date range specified in the "Calendar" table, even if there is no direct relationship between the two tables.

Tips:

- Use **TREATAS** when you need to apply filters from one table to another or when you want to override the filter context for specific calculations.

- Be mindful of the performance impact when using **TREATAS**, especially with large datasets. Overuse of this function can lead to slower query response times, so use it judiciously.

- Make sure there's a logical relationship between the columns used in the **TREATAS** function for it to work effectively.

The **TREATAS** function is a versatile tool for managing filter contexts and extending the capabilities of Power BI DAX calculations by allowing you to treat values as if they belong to a different column's filter context.

7. USERELATIONSHIP

Syntax:

USERELATIONSHIP(table_name[column_name],
related_table_name[related_column_name])

- `table_name[column_name]`: The column from the current table for which you want to specify a new relationship.

- `related_table_name[related_column_name]`: The column from the related table that you want to establish as the new relationship.

Description:

The **USERELATIONSHIP** function in Power BI DAX allows you to define a temporary, one-way relationship between tables for a specific calculation or measure. This function is particularly useful when there are multiple relationships between tables, and you need to choose which relationship to use for a specific context.

Example:

Imagine you have two tables: "Sales" and "Calendar." The "Sales" table contains sales transactions with a "TransactionDate" column, and the "Calendar" table includes a "Date" column. You have two relationships between these tables: one based on "TransactionDate" and another based on a "ShipDate." To calculate sales for a specific date range based on the "ShipDate" relationship, you can use the **USERELATIONSHIP** function.

DAX Formula:

SalesForSpecificDateRange =

  CALCULATE(

    SUM(Sales[Amount]),

    USERELATIONSHIP(Calendar[Date], Sales[ShipDate])

)

Result: The "SalesForSpecificDateRange" measure will sum the "Amount" column from the "Sales" table based on the relationship specified using **USERELATIONSHIP**, in this case, the "ShipDate" relationship.

Tips:

- Use **USERELATIONSHIP** when you need to override the default active relationship between tables for a specific calculation or measure. This function allows you to choose the desired relationship for a particular context.

- Be cautious when using **USERELATIONSHIP** as it can affect the behavior of other calculations in your model. Make sure to use it only when necessary.

- Ensure that there is a logical relationship between the columns you specify in **USERELATIONSHIP** for it to work effectively.

The **USERELATIONSHIP** function is a powerful tool for managing relationships in Power BI, giving you the flexibility to choose the appropriate relationship for different calculations and scenarios.

CHAPTER II
Formatting Functions

8. CONCATENATE

Syntax:

CONCATENATE(text1, [text2], ...)

- `text1`: The first text string or expression to concatenate.

- `[text2]`, `...`: Optional additional text strings or expressions to concatenate.

Description:

The **CONCATENATE** function in Power BI DAX is used to combine multiple text strings or expressions into a single text string. It allows you to merge text from different sources, add separators, or create custom labels for your data.

Example:

Suppose you have a table called "Employees" with columns "FirstName" and "LastName." You want to create a new column that combines these two columns into a single "FullName" column.

DAX Formula:

Employees[FullName] = CONCATENATE(Employees[FirstName], " ",
Employees[LastName])

Result: The "FullName" column will contain the full names of employees, combining the first name and last name with a space in between.

Tips:

- You can use CONCATENATE to join not only text strings but also numbers, dates, or any other data types. The function will automatically convert them to text before concatenation.

- To insert a separator (e.g., a comma or a hyphen) between concatenated items, you can include it as a text string in the formula. For example, `CONCATENATE("First Name: ", Employees[FirstName])` would include "First Name: " before the employee's first name.

- If you're concatenating a large number of text strings, consider using the "&" operator instead of **CONCATENATE** for improved performance and readability. For example, `Employees[FirstName] & " " & Employees[LastName]` achieves the same result as the example above.

The **CONCATENATE** function is a versatile tool for creating custom text expressions and combining text values within your Power BI reports and data models. It helps you format and label your data effectively for presentation and analysis.

9. FIXED

Syntax:

FIXED(number, [decimals], [comma])

- `number`: The number you want to format.

- `[decimals]`: Optional. The number of decimal places to display. Default is 2.

- `[comma]`: Optional. A boolean value (TRUE or FALSE) that determines whether to use a comma as a thousands separator. Default is FALSE.

Description:

The **FIXED** function in Power BI DAX is used to format a number as text with a specified number of decimal places and optional thousands separators. It is particularly helpful when you need to present numerical data in a more human-readable format, such as currency or percentages.

Example:

Suppose you have a measure called "AverageRevenue" that calculates the average revenue per customer. To format this measure with two decimal places and a comma as a thousands separator, you can use the **FIXED** function.

DAX Formula:

FormattedAverageRevenue = FIXED([AverageRevenue], 2, TRUE)

Result: The "FormattedAverageRevenue" measure will display the average revenue with two decimal places and thousands separated by commas, making it easier to read, e.g., "$1,234.56."

Tips:

- Use **FIXED** when you want to control the formatting of numbers for presentation purposes. It ensures consistent display regardless of the source data's precision.

- The `[decimals]` parameter allows you to specify how many decimal places you want to display. If omitted, it defaults to 2.

- The `[comma]` parameter, when set to TRUE, inserts commas as thousands separators, enhancing readability for large numbers.

- Be mindful of the formatting's impact on calculations. While **FIXED** changes the visual representation of a number, the underlying data remains unchanged. Perform calculations before applying formatting if necessary.

The **FIXED** function is a valuable tool for improving the readability of numerical data in your Power BI reports and dashboards, ensuring a clear and professional presentation of your insights.

10.FORMAT

Syntax:

FORMAT(expression, format_text)

- `expression`: The value or expression you want to format.

- `format_text`: A text string specifying the desired format for the expression.

Description:

The **FORMAT** function in Power BI DAX is used to format a value or expression into a text string based on a specified format. It allows you to control the display format of dates, times, numbers, and other data types in your reports and visuals.

Example:

Suppose you have a date column named "OrderDate" in your dataset, and you want to display it in a custom date format. You can use the FORMAT function to achieve this:

DAX Formula:

FormattedDate = FORMAT('Sales'[OrderDate], "dd-MM-yyyy")

Result: The "FormattedDate" column will display the "OrderDate" values in the format "dd-MM-yyyy," which represents the day, month, and year in a custom format (e.g., "05-09-2023").

Tips:

- Use the **FORMAT** function when you need precise control over the display format of values in your visuals. It is particularly useful for formatting dates, times, currency, and numbers according to specific preferences.

- The `format_text` parameter follows .NET Framework formatting patterns. You can find various format options and patterns in the official Microsoft documentation to customize your display.

- Be cautious when formatting values, especially for calculations. The **FORMAT** function converts values into text, so avoid using it for values that need to be used in further numeric calculations.

- Ensure that the `format_text` parameter matches the data type of the expression you are formatting. Using an incompatible format may result in unexpected outcomes.

The **FORMAT** function empowers you to control the visual representation of your data in Power BI reports, making it easier to convey information to your audience with precision and clarity.

11.INT

Syntax:

INT(number)

- `number`: The number you want to convert to an integer.

Description:

The INT function in Power BI DAX is used to convert a number into an integer by removing its decimal part. It rounds down the number to the nearest whole number towards negative infinity.

Example:

Suppose you have a column named "Price" in your dataset that contains product prices, including decimal values. You want to create a new column that represents these prices as whole numbers without decimals. You can use the **INT** function to achieve this:

DAX Formula:

IntegerPrice = INT('Products'[Price])

Result: The "IntegerPrice" column will contain the product prices as integers, effectively removing the decimal part. For example, a price of 19.99 will become 19.

Tips:

- Use the **INT** function when you need to eliminate decimal values from a number to work with whole numbers.

- Be aware that **INT** always rounds down towards negative infinity. This means that if you have a negative number with a decimal part, **INT** will make it more negative. For example, INT(-3.8) results in -4.

- Ensure that the column or measure you apply the **INT** function to contains numeric values. Using **INT** on non-numeric data may result in errors.

- When working with currency values, consider using **ROUND** or other rounding functions to round to the nearest integer, which might be more suitable in some scenarios.

The **INT** function is a handy tool for transforming numeric data in Power BI, particularly when you need to work with whole numbers and remove decimal portions for analysis and visualization.

12. REPT

Syntax:

REPT(text, number_of_times)

- `text`: The text or string you want to repeat.

- `number_of_times`: The number of times you want to repeat the text.

Description:

The **REPT** function in Power BI DAX is used to repeat a specified text or string a certain number of times and return the concatenated result. It's particularly useful for generating repetitive text patterns or creating visual elements in your reports.

Example:

Suppose you want to create a column that displays a star rating based on a numeric rating value in your dataset. You can use the **REPT** function to generate star icons based on the rating value:

DAX Formula:

StarRating = REPT("★", 'Product'[Rating])

Result: The "StarRating" column will contain star icons (★) repeated based on the "Rating" value. For example, if the rating is 4, you'll see "★★★★" in the column.

Tips:

- Use the **REPT** function when you need to generate repetitive text patterns, such as stars, dashes, or any other character, based on a numeric value.

- Ensure that the `text` parameter is a single character or string that you want to repeat. The function will repeat this character or string `number_of_times` times.

- Be mindful of the potential length of the result when using **REPT** with a large `number_of_times` value, as it can impact the visual representation and layout of your reports.

- You can combine **REPT** with other DAX functions or measures to create dynamic visual elements in your Power BI reports.

The **REPT** function is a valuable tool for creating repetitive text patterns and enhancing the visual appeal of your reports and dashboards by dynamically generating text-based visual elements based on data values.

13. ROUND

Syntax:

ROUND(number, num_digits)

- `number`: The number you want to round.

- `num_digits`: The number of decimal places to which you want to round the `number`. It can be positive (rounds to the right of the decimal point) or negative (rounds to the left of the decimal point).

Description:

The **ROUND** function in Power BI DAX is used to round a number to a specified number of decimal places. It can be used to adjust the precision of numerical values in your calculations or visualizations.

Example:

Suppose you have a column named "TaxRate" in your dataset that contains tax rates with several decimal places, and you want to round them to two decimal places for display:

DAX Formula:

RoundedTaxRate = ROUND('Sales'[TaxRate], 2)

Result: The "RoundedTaxRate" column will contain the tax rates rounded to two decimal places. For example, if the original tax rate is 0.0867, it will be rounded to 0.09.

Tips:

- Use the **ROUND** function when you need to adjust the precision of numeric values in your calculations or visualizations, such as when dealing with currency, percentages, or any situation where a specific number of decimal places is required.

- The `num_digits` parameter specifies the number of decimal places to which you want to round the number. If `num_digits` is positive, it rounds to the right of the decimal point; if negative, it rounds to the left of the decimal point.

- Be cautious when rounding numbers, as it can introduce rounding errors in calculations. Consider the impact of rounding on the accuracy of your results.

- If you need to truncate rather than round numbers, you can use the **TRUNC** function instead.

The **ROUND** function provides a straightforward way to adjust the precision of numerical values in Power BI, ensuring that your data is presented in the desired format for analysis and visualization.

14.TEXT

Syntax:

TEXT(value, format_text)

- `value`: The value or expression you want to format as text.

- `format_text`: A text string specifying the desired format for the value.

Description:

The **TEXT** function in Power BI DAX is used to format a value or expression into a text string based on a specified format. It is particularly useful for customizing the display format of dates, times, numbers, and other data types in your reports and visuals.

Example:

Suppose you have a date column named "OrderDate" in your dataset, and you want to create a new column that displays these dates in a custom date format. You can use the **TEXT** function to achieve this:

DAX Formula:

FormattedDate = TEXT('Sales'[OrderDate], "dd-MM-yyyy")

Result: The "FormattedDate" column will display the "OrderDate" values in the format "dd-MM-yyyy," representing the day, month, and year in a custom format (e.g., "05-09-2023").

Tips:

- Use the **TEXT** function when you need precise control over the display format of values in your visuals. It is particularly useful for formatting dates, times, currency, and numbers according to specific preferences.

- The `format_text` parameter follows .NET Framework formatting patterns. You can find various format options and patterns in the official Microsoft documentation to customize your display.

- Be cautious when formatting values, especially for calculations. The **TEXT** function converts values into text, so avoid using it for values that need to be used in further numeric calculations.

- Ensure that the `format_text` parameter matches the data type of the expression you are formatting. Using an incompatible format may result in unexpected outcomes.

The **TEXT** function empowers you to control the visual representation of your data in Power BI reports, making it easier to convey information to your audience with precision and clarity.

15. TIME

Syntax:

TIME(hour, minute, second)

- `hour`: The hour component of the time.

- `minute`: The minute component of the time.

- `second`: The second component of the time.

Description:

The **TIME** function in Power BI DAX is used to create a time value based on the specified hour, minute, and second components. It allows you to represent and work with time-related data in your calculations and visuals.

Example:

Suppose you have a dataset that includes two columns, "Hour" and "Minute," representing the hour and minute components of a time. You want to create a new column that combines these components to represent the time. You can use the TIME function as follows:

DAX Formula:

TimeValue = TIME('Table'[Hour], 'Table'[Minute], 0)

Result: The "TimeValue" column will contain time values based on the "Hour" and "Minute" components. For example, if "Hour" is 14 and "Minute" is 30, the column will display "14:30:00."

Tips:

- Use the **TIME** function when you need to create time values from separate hour, minute, and second components.

- Ensure that the values provided for "hour," "minute," and "second" are within valid ranges. Hours should be between 0 and 23, minutes between 0 and 59, and seconds between 0 and 59.

- If you don't have seconds information or want to represent a whole minute, you can set the "second" parameter to 0, as shown in the example.

- Time values created using the **TIME** function can be used in various time-related calculations and visualizations in Power BI.

The **TIME** function is a valuable tool for working with time-related data in Power BI, enabling you to create and manipulate time values for accurate reporting and analysis.

16. TRUNC

Syntax:

TRUNC(number, [num_digits])

- `number`: The number you want to truncate.

- `[num_digits]`: Optional. The number of decimal places to which you want to truncate the `number`. If omitted, it defaults to 0.

Description:

The **TRUNC** function in Power BI DAX is used to truncate a number to a specified number of decimal places or to remove the decimal part altogether. It effectively rounds the number towards zero.

Example:

Suppose you have a column named "Temperature" in your dataset that contains temperature readings with several decimal places, and you want to truncate them to whole numbers for display:

DAX Formula:

TruncatedTemperature = TRUNC('Weather'[Temperature])

Result: The "TruncatedTemperature" column will contain the temperature values truncated to whole numbers. For example, if the original temperature is 23.987, it will be truncated to 23.

Tips:

- Use the **TRUNC** function when you need to remove the decimal portion of a number or round it to a specific number of decimal places.

- The `[num_digits]` parameter specifies the number of decimal places to which you want to truncate the number. If omitted, it defaults to 0, resulting in the removal of the decimal part.

- Be cautious when truncating numbers, as it may lead to loss of precision. Consider the impact of truncation on the accuracy of your results.

- Unlike the **ROUND** function, which rounds numbers to the nearest value, **TRUNC** always rounds towards zero, effectively eliminating the decimal part.

The **TRUNC** function is a useful tool for adjusting the precision of numerical values in Power BI, particularly when you need to work with whole numbers or remove decimal portions for analysis   and   visualization.

CHAPTER III
Positioning Functions

17.EARLIER

Syntax:

EARLIER([column_name])

- `[column_name]`: Optional. The name of a column or measure from the current row context that you want to refer to using an earlier row context.

Description:

The **EARLIER** function in Power BI DAX is used to refer to a column or measure from an earlier row context within an iteration. It is often used in calculated columns or measures to compare or perform calculations with values from a previous row.

Example:

Suppose you have a table with sales transactions, and you want to create a calculated column that calculates the difference between the current transaction's sales amount and the sales amount of the previous transaction. You can use the **EARLIER** function to refer to the sales amount of the previous row:

DAX Formula:

SalesDifference = 'Sales'[SalesAmount] - EARLIER('Sales'[SalesAmount])

Result: The "SalesDifference" column will contain the difference between the current transaction's sales amount and the sales amount of the previous transaction. For example, if the current transaction has a sales amount of $500, and the previous transaction had a sales amount of $400, the column will display $100.

Tips:

- Use the **EARLIER** function when you need to refer to a column or measure from an earlier row context within an iteration. It is particularly useful for creating calculated columns or measures that involve comparisons with previous values.

- You can optionally specify the `[column_name]` parameter to explicitly indicate the column or measure you want to refer to. If omitted, **EARLIER** will refer to the entire row context.

- Be cautious when using **EARLIER** in complex calculations, as it may lead to performance issues in large datasets. It's essential to optimize your data model and calculations for efficiency.

- The **EARLIER** function is particularly valuable when working with time-series data or data that requires comparisons between consecutive rows.

The **EARLIER** function provides a way to access values from previous row contexts within your Power BI calculations, allowing you to create dynamic and context-aware measures and calculated columns.

18. FIRSTNONBLANK

Syntax:

FIRSTNONBLANK(table, expression[, skip_values])

- `table`: The table to evaluate.

- `expression`: The expression to evaluate in the table context.

- `[skip_values]`: Optional. The values to skip when evaluating the expression.

Description:

The **FIRSTNONBLANK** function in Power BI DAX is used to find the first non-blank value in a table when evaluating a given expression. It helps identify the earliest non-blank data point based on the specified criteria.

Example:

Suppose you have a table named "Sales" with columns "Date" and "Revenue," and you want to find the first date with non-zero revenue. You can use the FIRSTNONBLANK function as follows:

DAX Formula:

FirstDateWithRevenue = FIRSTNONBLANK('Sales', 'Sales'[Date], 'Sales'[Revenue] > 0)

Result: The "FirstDateWithRevenue" value will be the date of the first non-zero revenue in the "Sales" table.

Tips:

- Use the **FIRSTNONBLANK** function when you need to identify the earliest data point in a table that satisfies specific criteria, especially in time-based or sequential data analysis.

- The `table` parameter specifies the table to evaluate, and the `expression` parameter is the column or measure to evaluate in the table context.

- You can optionally provide the `[skip_values]` parameter to skip specific values when evaluating the expression. For example, you can skip zero values or other specific values to find the first non-blank value that meets your criteria.

- Be cautious when using **FIRSTNONBLANK** in complex data models with large datasets, as it may impact performance. Ensure that your data model is optimized for efficiency.

The **FIRSTNONBLANK** function is a valuable tool for identifying the earliest non-blank data point in a table based on specific criteria, making it useful for various analytical scenarios in Power BI.

19.FIRSTNONBLANKVALUE

Syntax:

FIRSTNONBLANKVALUE(table, expression[, skip_values[, alternate_result]])

- `table`: The table to evaluate.

- `expression`: The expression to evaluate in the table context.

- `[skip_values]`: Optional. The values to skip when evaluating the expression.

- `[alternate_result]`: Optional. The value to return if there are no non-blank values that meet the criteria.

Description:

The **FIRSTNONBLANKVALUE** function in Power BI DAX is used to find the first non-blank value in a table when evaluating a given expression. It helps identify the earliest non-blank data point based on the specified criteria and provides an optional alternate result if no such value is found.

Example:

Suppose you have a table named "Sales" with columns "Date" and "Revenue," and you want to find the first date with non-zero revenue. You can use the FIRSTNONBLANKVALUE function as follows:

DAX Formula:

FirstDateWithRevenue = FIRSTNONBLANKVALUE('Sales', 'Sales'[Date], 'Sales'[Revenue] > 0, BLANK())

Result: The "FirstDateWithRevenue" value will be the date of the first non-zero revenue in the "Sales" table. If no such date is found, it will return a blank value.

Tips:

- Use the **FIRSTNONBLANKVALUE** function when you need to identify the earliest data point in a table that satisfies specific criteria, especially in time-based or sequential data analysis. It offers the flexibility to provide an alternate result if no matching non-blank value is found.

- The `table` parameter specifies the table to evaluate, and the `expression` parameter is the column or measure to evaluate in the table context.

- You can optionally provide the `[skip_values]` parameter to skip specific values when evaluating the expression. For example, you can skip zero values or other specific values to find the first non-blank value that meets your criteria.

- The `[alternate_result]` parameter allows you to specify a value to return if no non-blank values meet the criteria. This can be helpful for handling cases where no matching data point is found.

- Be cautious when using **FIRSTNONBLANKVALUE** in complex data models with large datasets, as it may impact performance. Ensure that your data model is optimized for efficiency.

The **FIRSTNONBLANKVALUE** function is a versatile tool for identifying the earliest non-blank data point in a table based on specific criteria, with the added benefit of handling cases where no matching data point exists by providing an alternate result. This makes it valuable for various analytical scenarios in Power BI.

20.LASTNONBLANK

Syntax:

LASTNONBLANK(table, expression[, skip_values[, alternate_result]])

- `table`: The table to evaluate.

- `expression`: The expression to evaluate in the table context.

- `[skip_values]`: Optional. The values to skip when evaluating the expression.

- `[alternate_result]`: Optional. The value to return if there are no non-blank values that meet the criteria.

Description:

The **LASTNONBLANK** function in Power BI DAX is used to find the last non-blank value in a table when evaluating a given expression. It helps identify the most recent non-blank data point based on the specified criteria and provides an optional alternate result if no such value is found.

Example:

Suppose you have a table named "Sales" with columns "Date" and "Revenue," and you want to find the last date with non-zero revenue. You can use the LASTNONBLANK function as follows:

DAX Formula:

LastDateWithRevenue = LASTNONBLANK('Sales', 'Sales'[Date], 'Sales'[Revenue] > 0, BLANK())

Result: The "LastDateWithRevenue" value will be the date of the last non-zero revenue in the "Sales" table. If no such date is found, it will return a blank value.

Tips:

- Use the **LASTNONBLANK** function when you need to identify the most recent data point in a table that satisfies specific criteria, especially in time-based or sequential data analysis. It offers the flexibility to provide an alternate result if no matching non-blank value is found.

- The `table` parameter specifies the table to evaluate, and the `expression` parameter is the column or measure to evaluate in the table context.

- You can optionally provide the `[skip_values]` parameter to skip specific values when evaluating the expression. For example, you can skip zero values or other specific values to find the last non-blank value that meets your criteria.

- The `[alternate_result]` parameter allows you to specify a value to return if no non-blank values meet the criteria. This can be helpful for handling cases where no matching data point is found.

- Be cautious when using **LASTNONBLANK** in complex data models with large datasets, as it may impact performance. Ensure that your data model is optimized for efficiency.

The **LASTNONBLANK** function is a versatile tool for identifying the most recent non-blank data point in a table based on specific criteria, with the added benefit of handling cases where no matching data point exists by providing an alternate result. This makes it valuable for various analytical scenarios in Power BI.

21.LASTNONBLANKVALUE

Syntax:

LASTNONBLANKVALUE(table, expression[, skip_values[, alternate_result]])

- `table`: The table to evaluate.

- `expression`: The expression to evaluate in the table context.

- `[skip_values]`: Optional. The values to skip when evaluating the expression.

- `[alternate_result]`: Optional. The value to return if there are no non-blank values that meet the criteria.

Description:

The **LASTNONBLANKVALUE** function in Power BI DAX is used to find the last non-blank value in a table when evaluating a given expression. It helps identify the most recent non-blank data point based on the specified criteria and provides an optional alternate result if no such value is found.

Example:

Suppose you have a table named "Sales" with columns "Date" and "Revenue," and you want to find the last date with non-zero revenue. You can use the **LASTNONBLANKVALUE** function as follows:

DAX Formula:

LastDateWithRevenue = LASTNONBLANKVALUE('Sales', 'Sales'[Date], 'Sales'[Revenue] > 0, BLANK())

Result: The "LastDateWithRevenue" value will be the date of the last non-zero revenue in the "Sales" table. If no such date is found, it will return a blank value.

Tips:

- Use the **LASTNONBLANKVALUE** function when you need to identify the most recent data point in a table that satisfies specific criteria, especially in time-based or sequential data analysis. It offers the flexibility to provide an alternate result if no matching non-blank value is found.

- The `table` parameter specifies the table to evaluate, and the `expression` parameter is the column or measure to evaluate in the table context.

- You can optionally provide the `[skip_values]` parameter to skip specific values when evaluating the expression. For example, you can skip zero values or other specific values to find the last non-blank value that meets your criteria.

- The `[alternate_result]` parameter allows you to specify a value to return if no non-blank values meet the criteria. This can be helpful for handling cases where no matching data point is found.

- Be cautious when using **LASTNONBLANKVALUE** in complex data models with large datasets, as it may impact performance. Ensure that your data model is optimized for efficiency.

The **LASTNONBLANKVALUE** function is a versatile tool for identifying the most recent non-blank data point in a table based on specific criteria, with the added benefit of handling cases where no matching data point exists by providing an alternate result. This makes it valuable for various analytical scenarios in Power BI.

22.LOOKUPVALUE

Syntax:

LOOKUPVALUE(result_column, search_column, search_value[, alternate_result])

- `result_column`: The column from which you want to retrieve the result.

- `search_column`: The column in which to search for the `search_value`.

- `search_value`: The value to search for in the `search_column`.

- `[alternate_result]`: Optional. The value to return if no matching value is found.

Description:

The **LOOKUPVALUE** function in Power BI DAX is used to search for a specific value in a column and retrieve a related value from another column in the same table. It is helpful for performing lookup operations based on criteria and can provide an alternate result if no match is found.

Example:

Suppose you have a table named "Products" with columns "ProductID" and "ProductName," and you want to find the name of a product based on its ID. You can use the LOOKUPVALUE function as follows:

DAX Formula:

ProductName = LOOKUPVALUE('Products'[ProductName], 'Products'[ProductID], 101)

Result: The "ProductName" value will be the name of the product with the ID 101, such as "Widget A."

Tips:

- Use the **LOOKUPVALUE** function when you need to search for a specific value in a column and retrieve a related value from another column. It is particularly useful for creating calculated columns or measures that involve lookups based on certain criteria.

- The `result_column` parameter specifies the column from which you want to retrieve the result, while the `search_column` and `search_value` parameters define the search criteria.

- You can optionally provide the `[alternate_result]` parameter to specify a value to return if no matching value is found. This can be useful for handling cases where no match exists.

- Be cautious when using **LOOKUPVALUE** in large datasets or complex data models, as it may impact performance. Ensure that your data model is optimized for efficiency.

The **LOOKUPVALUE** function simplifies the process of performing lookups and retrieving related values in Power BI, making it a valuable tool for data analysis and reporting.

23. PERCENTRANKX.INC

Syntax:

PERCENTRANKX.INC(table, expression, value[, significance])

- `table`: The table to evaluate.

- `expression`: The expression to evaluate in the table context.

- `value`: The value for which you want to calculate the percentile rank.

- `[significance]`: Optional. A significance level between 0 and 1 (inclusive) that specifies the interpolation method. The default is 0, which corresponds to exclusive interpolation.

Description:

The **PERCENTRANKX.INC** function in Power BI DAX is used to calculate the percentile rank of a given value within a table column, considering all rows that match the expression. It returns a value between 0 and 1, indicating the relative rank of the value compared to the values in the column.

Example:

Suppose you have a table named "Sales" with a column "Revenue" and you want to calculate the percentile rank of a specific revenue value, say $5,000, among all the sales records:

DAX Formula:

PercentileRank = PERCENTRANKX.INC('Sales', 'Sales'[Revenue], 5000)

Result: The "PercentileRank" value will be the percentile rank of $5,000 within the "Revenue" column of the "Sales" table. This value indicates where $5,000 ranks relative to all the revenue values in the table.

Tips:

- Use the **PERCENTRANKX.INC** function when you need to determine the percentile rank of a specific value within a table column. It is commonly used for analyzing data distribution and identifying how a value compares to other values in the dataset.

- The `table` parameter specifies the table to evaluate, the `expression` parameter defines the column or measure to evaluate in the table context, and the `value` parameter is the value for which you want to calculate the percentile rank.

- The `[significance]` parameter allows you to control the interpolation method. A significance level of 0 (default) corresponds to exclusive interpolation, while a significance level of 1 corresponds to inclusive interpolation.

- The result of **PERCENTRANKX.INC** is a decimal value between 0 and 1, where 0 represents the lowest rank and 1 represents the highest rank. For example, a result of 0.7 means the value ranks higher than 70% of the values in the column.

- Be aware of the significance level you choose, as it can affect how percentile ranks are calculated, especially when multiple values have the same rank.

The **PERCENTRANKX.INC** function is a valuable tool for understanding the relative position of a value within a dataset, making it useful for various analytical and statistical tasks in Power BI.

24.RANKX

Syntax:

RANKX(table, expression[, value][, order][, tie])

- `table`: The table to evaluate.

- `expression`: The expression to evaluate in the table context.

- `[value]`: Optional. The value to rank within the table. If omitted, it ranks all values based on the expression.

- `[order]`: Optional. The order in which to rank values. It can be "asc" (ascending) or "desc" (descending). The default is "asc."

- `[tie]`: Optional. The tie-breaking method when values have the same rank. It can be "first," "last," or "average." The default is "average."

Description:

The **RANKX** function in Power BI DAX is used to calculate the rank of a specified value or all values within a table column based on a given expression. It assigns a numeric rank to each value, indicating its relative position within the dataset. You can control the ranking order and tie-breaking method.

Example:

Suppose you have a table named "Sales" with a column "Revenue" and you want to calculate the rank of a specific revenue value, say $10,000:

DAX Formula:

RankOf10000 = RANKX('Sales', 'Sales'[Revenue], 10000)

Result: The "RankOf10000" value will be the rank of $10,000 within the "Revenue" column of the "Sales" table. This rank indicates where $10,000 stands in relation to other revenue values.

Tips:

- Use the **RANKX** function when you need to assign a rank to values within a table column based on a specific expression. It is useful for creating rankings and understanding the relative positions of values in your data.

- The `table` parameter specifies the table to evaluate, the `expression` parameter defines the column or measure to evaluate in the table context, and the `[value]` parameter is optional and allows you to rank a specific value. If `[value]` is omitted, all values are ranked based on the expression.

- The `[order]` parameter controls the ranking order and can be set to "asc" (ascending) or "desc" (descending). The default is "asc."

- The `[tie]` parameter determines the tie-breaking method when multiple values have the same rank. It can be "first" (assigns the lowest rank to tied values), "last" (assigns the highest rank to tied values), or "average" (assigns an average rank to tied values). The default is "average."

- Be mindful of the ranking order and tie-breaking method you choose, as they can significantly impact the ranking results, especially when there are tied values.

The **RANKX** function is a versatile tool for creating customized rankings within your Power BI reports, allowing you to analyze and visualize data based on specific criteria and expressions.

CHAPTER IV
Data Modeling Functions

25.ADDCOLUMNS

Syntax:

ADDCOLUMNS(table, new_column_name, expression1[, new_column_name2, expression2, ...])

- `table`: The table to which you want to add columns.

- `new_column_name`: The name of the new column to be added.

- `expression1`: The DAX expression to calculate values for the new column.

- `new_column_name2`: Optional. The name of a second new column.

- `expression2`: Optional. The DAX expression for the second new column, if specified.

Description:

The **ADDCOLUMNS** function in Power BI DAX is used to add one or more new columns to a table by specifying their names and corresponding DAX expressions. You can use this function to create calculated columns on the fly, enhancing your data model with additional information.

Example:

Suppose you have a table named "Sales" with columns "Product" and "Quantity," and you want to create a new column that calculates the total revenue for each product by multiplying the quantity sold by the product's price. You can use the **ADDCOLUMNS** function as follows:

DAX Formula:

EnhancedSales = ADDCOLUMNS('Sales', "TotalRevenue", 'Sales'[Quantity] * 'Products'[Price])

Result: The "EnhancedSales" table will contain the original columns from "Sales" along with a new "TotalRevenue" column that contains the calculated total revenue for each product.

Tips:

- Use the **ADDCOLUMNS** function when you need to create new calculated columns based on existing columns or DAX expressions within a table. It is a powerful tool for enriching your data model with additional information for analysis.

- The `table` parameter specifies the table to which you want to add columns. You can use an existing table or the result of a DAX expression that produces a table.

- For each new column, provide a `new_column_name` and the corresponding `expression` to calculate values for that column.

- You can add multiple new columns in a single **ADDCOLUMNS** function call by providing pairs of `new_column_name` and `expression` arguments.

- Be mindful of the DAX expressions you use for creating new columns, as they can impact the performance and efficiency of your data model. Complex expressions may slow down query processing.

The **ADDCOLUMNS** function is a valuable feature for dynamically enhancing your Power BI data model with calculated columns, allowing you to perform more advanced analysis and reporting with ease.

26. ADDMISSINGITEMS

Syntax:

ADDMISSINGITEMS(table, column, new_item)

- `table`: The table to evaluate.

- `column`: The column to which you want to add missing items.

- `new_item`: The new item to add to the column for any missing values.

Description:

The **ADDMISSINGITEMS** function in Power BI DAX is used to add missing items to a column within a table. It ensures that all unique values in the specified column exist, and if a value is missing, it adds the provided `new_item` to the column for those missing values.

Example:

Suppose you have a table named "Products" with a column "Category" containing various product categories. Some products are missing a category, and you want to add the category "Uncategorized" to those products. You can use the **ADDMISSINGITEMS** function as follows:

DAX Formula:

EnhancedProducts = ADDMISSINGITEMS('Products', 'Category', "Uncategorized")

Result: The "EnhancedProducts" table will contain the same columns as the original "Products" table, but any products with missing categories will now have "Uncategorized" as their category.

Tips:

- Use the **ADDMISSINGITEMS** function when you need to ensure that a specific column within a table contains all necessary items, especially when working with categorical data or creating relationships between tables.

- The `table` parameter specifies the table to evaluate, the `column` parameter specifies the column to which you want to add missing items, and `new_item` is the value to add for any missing items.

- **ADDMISSINGITEMS** is particularly useful when you want to ensure data integrity and consistency in your data model by providing default values for missing items.

- Be cautious when using this function, as it can potentially impact the structure of your data model. Make sure that adding missing items aligns with your data analysis goals.

The **ADDMISSINGITEMS** function is a valuable tool for data preparation and data quality assurance, allowing you to handle missing or incomplete data gracefully and ensuring that your data model is comprehensive and accurate.

27.ALLCROSSFILTERED

Syntax:

ALLCROSSFILTERED(table)

- `table`: The table for which you want to apply cross-filtering context.

Description:

The **ALLCROSSFILTERED** function in Power BI DAX is used to remove cross-filtering from a specific table within a calculation. It returns a table that includes all the rows from the specified table but without any cross-filtering applied. This function is particularly useful when you want to ignore any filtering effects from related tables temporarily.

Example:

Suppose you have two tables, "Sales" and "Product," and there is a relationship between them. If you want to calculate the total sales for all products, ignoring any filters applied to the "Product" table, you can use the **ALLCROSSFILTERED** function as follows:

DAX Formula:

TotalSales = SUMX(ALLCROSSFILTERED('Product'), 'Sales'[Revenue])

Result: The "TotalSales" value will be the sum of revenue from the "Sales" table, considering all products in the "Product" table without any cross-filtering applied from "Product."

Tips:

- Use the **ALLCROSSFILTERED** function when you need to remove cross-filtering effects from a specific table within a DAX calculation. This allows you to create calculations that are not influenced by filters from related tables.

- The `table` parameter specifies the table for which you want to remove cross-filtering context. All rows from this table will be included in the result, regardless of any active filters from related tables.

- Be cautious when using **ALLCROSSFILTERED**, as it can potentially lead to unexpected results if not used carefully. Removing cross-filtering should be done deliberately and in scenarios where it makes sense for your analysis.

- Consider combining **ALLCROSSFILTERED** with other DAX functions to create complex calculations that consider specific contexts while ignoring cross-filtering effects.

The **ALLCROSSFILTERED** function is a valuable tool for controlling the impact of cross-filtering on your calculations and ensuring that your DAX measures behave as expected in various scenarios.

28. CALENDARAUTO

Syntax:

CALENDARAUTO()

Description:

The **CALENDARAUTO** function in Power BI DAX is a date and time intelligence function that generates a date table automatically based on the date columns present in the data model. It creates a dynamic calendar table with date hierarchies, allowing users to perform time-based analysis without the need to manually create a date table.

Example:

Suppose you have imported data into Power BI that includes a date column named "OrderDate," and you want to analyze your data using date-based calculations. Instead of manually creating a calendar table, you can use the **CALENDARAUTO** function as follows:

DAX Formula:

CalendarTable = CALENDARAUTO()

Result: The "CalendarTable" will be a dynamically generated date table with date hierarchies, including year, quarter, month, and day. It will automatically adjust to the date range in your data.

Tips:

- Use the **CALENDARAUTO** function when you want to create a date table on the fly without the need for manual setup. It simplifies the process of performing time-based analysis in Power BI.

- The **CALENDARAUTO** function analyzes the date columns present in your data model and generates a calendar table based on the date range found. It automatically detects the earliest and latest dates in your data.

- The generated calendar table includes pre-built hierarchies, making it easy to perform time-based aggregations and drill-downs in your reports and visualizations.

- Be aware that the **CALENDARAUTO** function creates a dynamic table, meaning it adapts to changes in your data. If your data source is updated with new date values, the calendar table will adjust accordingly.

- You can customize the generated calendar table further by adding calculated columns or modifying the date hierarchies to suit your specific reporting needs.

The **CALENDARAUTO** function is a time-saving feature in Power BI that simplifies the process of creating and maintaining date tables for time-based analysis, improving the efficiency of your data modeling and reporting tasks.

29.DATATABLE

Syntax:

DATATABLE(column1_name, datatype1, column2_name, datatype2, ...)

- `column1_name`: The name of the first column in the table.

- `datatype1`: The data type for the first column.

- `column2_name`: The name of the second column in the table.

- `datatype2`: The data type for the second column, and so on for additional columns.

Description:

The **DATATABLE** function in Power BI DAX is used to create a table with custom-defined columns and data types. It allows you to specify the structure of the table, including column names and data types, and populate it with data values. This function is commonly used to create small lookup tables or tables for testing and experimentation.

Example:

Suppose you want to create a simple table named "Employee" with two columns, "EmployeeID" and "EmployeeName," using the **DATATABLE** function:

DAX Formula:

```
Employee = DATATABLE(
    "EmployeeID", INTEGER,
    "EmployeeName", STRING,
    { {1, "John"}, {2, "Jane"}, {3, "Alice"} }
)
```

Result: The "Employee" table will be created with the specified columns and data types. It will contain three rows of data, representing employee IDs and names.

Tips:

- Use the **DATATABLE** function when you need to create custom tables with predefined column structures and data types. It is particularly useful for creating small lookup tables or tables for testing and development.

- Specify column names and data types in pairs within the **DATATABLE** function. You can create as many columns as needed by providing alternating column names and data types.

- Populate the table with data values by enclosing rows of data in curly braces `{}` within the function. Each set of curly braces represents a row, and the values within the braces represent the column values.

- The data types supported by **DATATABLE** include INTEGER, STRING, BOOLEAN, DECIMAL, CURRENCY, DATE, DATETIME, and more.

- You can use the tables created with **DATATABLE** in your DAX calculations, join them with other tables, or use them for specific analysis purposes within your Power BI reports.

The **DATATABLE** function is a versatile tool for creating custom tables tailored to your data modeling needs in Power BI. It provides flexibility in defining table structures and data types, allowing you to effectively work with data in your reports and analyses.

30.DETAILROWS

Syntax:

DETAILROWS(table)

- `table`: The table or table expression for which you want to retrieve detailed rows.

Description:

The **DETAILROWS** function in Power BI DAX is used to retrieve the detailed rows from a table or table expression that is the result of a specific calculation or filter context. It allows you to drill down into the details of a specific calculation or filtering condition, providing a more granular view of the data.

Example:

Suppose you have a table named "Sales" and a measure named "Total Sales," which calculates the sum of sales revenue. If you want to see the individual sales transactions that contribute to the "Total Sales" measure, you can use the DETAILROWS function as follows:

DAX Formula:

DetailedSales = DETAILROWS('Sales')

Result: The "DetailedSales" table will contain all the individual sales transactions that make up the "Total Sales" measure. It provides a detailed view of the underlying data contributing to the calculation.

Tips:

- Use the **DETAILROWS** function when you want to see the detailed rows that contribute to a specific calculation or filter context. It is particularly useful for data exploration and understanding the source of aggregated measures.

- The `table` parameter specifies the table or table expression for which you want to retrieve detailed rows. This table should be a result of a calculation or filter context that you want to examine in more detail.

- The **DETAILROWS** function is often used in combination with measures to gain insights into the specific data points that affect the measure's result. It helps you understand how the measure is calculated and the impact of filtering conditions.

- Be cautious when using **DETAILROWS** with large datasets, as it can generate a substantial amount of detailed data, potentially affecting performance.

- Consider using **DETAILROWS** in combination with other DAX functions and visuals to create interactive reports that allow users to drill down into specific data points.

The **DETAILROWS** function is a valuable tool for exploring and visualizing detailed data within the context of calculated measures, providing a more comprehensive understanding of your data and its contributions to your analyses in Power BI.

31.EVALUATE

Syntax:

EVALUATE

{ <TableExpression1> }

{ <TableExpression2> }

...

- `<TableExpression1>`, `<TableExpression2>`, ...: One or more table expressions to be evaluated.

Description:

The **EVALUATE** function in Power BI DAX is used in Data Analysis Expressions (DAX) queries to retrieve and manipulate data from tables. It is commonly used in DAX queries to specify one or more table expressions to be evaluated, and the results are returned as a table.

Example:

Suppose you have a table named "Sales" with columns "Product" and "Revenue," and you want to retrieve all the products with revenue greater than $1,000. You can use the EVALUATE function in a DAX query as follows:

DAX Query:

EVALUATE

FILTER('Sales', 'Sales'[Revenue] > 1000)

Result: The result of the DAX query will be a table containing all the rows from the "Sales" table where the revenue is greater than $1,000.

Tips:

- Use the **EVALUATE** function when you need to perform data retrieval and manipulation in DAX queries. It allows you to specify table expressions and apply filters, calculations, or other operations.

- Within the **EVALUATE** block, you can specify one or more table expressions enclosed in curly braces `{}`. These expressions can include filter conditions, calculations, or other operations on tables.

- The result of the **EVALUATE** function is always a table, making it suitable for returning filtered or transformed data sets in your DAX queries.

- You can combine **EVALUATE** with other DAX functions and operators to create more complex queries and perform various data analysis tasks.

- Remember that DAX queries and the **EVALUATE** function are typically used in Power BI Desktop's Query Editor or DAX Studio to retrieve and manipulate data from your data model.

The **EVALUATE** function is a fundamental tool in Power BI DAX for performing data analysis and extraction tasks through DAX queries. It provides the flexibility to work with data in a tabular format and is commonly used for various reporting and analysis needs.

32. EXCEPT

Syntax:

EXCEPT(Table1, Table2)

- `Table1`: The first table or table expression.

- `Table2`: The second table or table expression.

Description:

The **EXCEPT** function in Power BI DAX is used to return a table that contains all the rows from the first table (`Table1`) except for the rows that also exist in the second table (`Table2`). It effectively removes common rows between the two tables, keeping only the unique rows from `Table1`.

Example:

Suppose you have two tables, "Employees" and "Managers," both containing a column named "EmployeeID." If you want to retrieve a list of employees who are not also managers, you can use the **EXCEPT** function as follows:

DAX Formula:

NonManagers = EXCEPT('Employees', 'Managers')

Result: The "NonManagers" table will contain all the employees from the "Employees" table except for those who are also listed in the "Managers" table.

Tips:

- Use the **EXCEPT** function when you need to find the difference between two tables by removing common rows. It is helpful for identifying unique or non-overlapping data points.

- The first parameter, `Table1`, specifies the source table from which you want to exclude rows. The second parameter, `Table2`, provides the table whose rows you want to remove from `Table1`.

- The result of the **EXCEPT** function is a table that includes all the columns from `Table1`. The columns should have the same name and data type in both tables.

- You can use the **EXCEPT** function in various scenarios, such as finding missing or unique records, filtering out unwanted data, or creating custom data sets.

- Be mindful of column names and data types when using **EXCEPT**. The tables being compared should have compatible column structures.

- Consider using the **EXCEPT** function in combination with other DAX functions or visualization tools to analyze and display data differences effectively.

The **EXCEPT** function is a powerful tool for comparing and manipulating tables in Power BI DAX, allowing you to identify unique or distinct data points and create custom data sets for your analysis and reporting needs.

33.GROUPBY

Syntax:

GROUPBY(

    table,

    grouping_column1, [grouping_column2, ...],

    aggregation_expression1, [aggregation_expression2, ...]

)

- `table`: The table or table expression you want to group.

- `grouping_column1`, `grouping_column2`, ...: Columns by which you want to group the data.

- `aggregation_expression1`, `aggregation_expression2`, ...: Aggregation expressions for calculating aggregated values within each group.

Description:

The **GROUPBY** function in Power BI DAX is used to group rows from a table based on one or more columns and perform aggregation operations on the grouped data. It allows you to create summarized tables or calculate aggregated values within specific groups.

Example:

Suppose you have a table named "Sales" with columns "Product," "Category," and "Revenue," and you want to group the sales data by "Category" and calculate the total revenue for each category. You can use the **GROUPBY** function as follows:

DAX Formula:

CategoryRevenue =

GROUPBY(

   'Sales',

   'Sales'[Category],

   "TotalRevenue", SUM('Sales'[Revenue])

)

Result: The "CategoryRevenue" table will be created with two columns: "Category" and "TotalRevenue." It will contain one row for each unique category in the "Sales" table, and the "TotalRevenue" column will show the sum of revenue for each category.

Tips:

- Use the **GROUPBY** function when you need to group rows in a table based on one or more columns and perform aggregations within each group. It is commonly used for creating summary tables or calculating group-level statistics.

- Specify the `table` parameter as the source table you want to group. Provide one or more `grouping_column` parameters to define the columns by which you want to group the data.

- Use `aggregation_expression` parameters to specify the aggregation operations you want to perform within each group. Common aggregation functions include SUM, COUNT, AVERAGE, MAX, MIN, etc.

- The result of the **GROUPBY** function is a new table that contains the grouped data and calculated aggregations. The columns in the result table include the grouping columns and the calculated aggregation columns.

- You can use the resulting table in visuals or further calculations to analyze and visualize the summarized data.

- Experiment with different aggregation expressions and grouping columns to create customized summaries of your data that meet your reporting needs.

The **GROUPBY** function is a valuable tool in Power BI DAX for summarizing and aggregating data, enabling you to gain insights into your data by examining group-level statistics and creating informative reports and visuals.

34. INTERSECT

Syntax:

INTERSECT(Table1, Table2)

- `Table1`: The first table or table expression.

- `Table2`: The second table or table expression.

Description:

The **INTERSECT** function in Power BI DAX is used to return a table that contains only the rows that exist in both `Table1` and `Table2`. It effectively identifies the common rows between two tables, creating an intersection of the data.

Example:

Suppose you have two tables, "Customers" and "VIPCustomers," both containing a list of customer names. If you want to find the names of customers who are both in the "Customers" and "VIPCustomers" tables, you can use the **INTERSECT** function as follows:

DAX Formula:

CommonCustomers = INTERSECT('Customers', 'VIPCustomers')

Result: The "CommonCustomers" table will contain the names of customers who appear in both the "Customers" and "VIPCustomers" tables.

Tips:

- Use the **INTERSECT** function when you need to identify and retrieve common rows between two tables. It is useful for finding overlapping or shared data points.

- Both `Table1` and `Table2` parameters should specify tables or table expressions that have the same structure, including column names and data types.

- The result of the **INTERSECT** function is a table that includes all columns from `Table1`. The resulting table contains only the rows that exist in both input tables.

- You can use the **INTERSECT** function to perform set operations and identify shared data points within your data model.

- Be cautious when using **INTERSECT** with large datasets, as it may generate a substantial amount of data if there are many common rows.

- Consider combining **INTERSECT** with other DAX functions or visualization tools to analyze and visualize the intersection of data effectively.

The **INTERSECT** function is a valuable tool for identifying common data points between two tables in Power BI DAX, allowing you to perform set operations and gain insights into shared data within your data model.

35.NATURALINNERJOIN

Syntax:

NATURALINNERJOIN(Table1, Table2)

- `Table1`: The first table or table expression.

- `Table2`: The second table or table expression.

Description:

The **NATURALINNERJOIN** function in Power BI DAX is used to return a new table that contains the rows from `Table1` that have matching values in common columns with `Table2`. It performs an inner join operation based on columns with the same name and data type in both tables, creating an intersection of the data.

Example:

Suppose you have two tables, "Employees" and "Departments," both containing columns "EmployeeID" and "DepartmentID." If you want to find employees who are associated with a department by matching their "EmployeeID" with the "DepartmentID" in the "Departments" table, you can use the **NATURALINNERJOIN** function as follows:

DAX Formula:

EmployeeDepartment = NATURALINNERJOIN('Employees', 'Departments')

Result: The "EmployeeDepartment" table will contain the rows from the "Employees" table that have matching "EmployeeID" values in the "Departments" table. It effectively associates employees with their respective departments.

Tips:

- Use the **NATURALINNERJOIN** function when you want to perform an inner join operation between two tables based on common column names and data types. It simplifies the join process when tables share similar columns.

- The columns used for the join should have the same name and data type in both tables. **NATURALINNERJOIN** performs the join operation based on these matching columns.

- The result of the **NATURALINNERJOIN** function is a new table that includes columns from both `Table1` and `Table2`. The resulting table contains rows with matching values in the common columns.

- This function is particularly useful when dealing with related data, such as associating employees with departments or customers with orders.

- Be cautious when using **NATURALINNERJOIN** with large datasets, as it may generate a substantial amount of data if there are many common rows.

- Consider combining **NATURALINNERJOIN** with other DAX functions and visualization tools to perform more advanced data analysis and reporting.

The **NATURALINNERJOIN** function simplifies the process of joining tables in Power BI DAX by automatically identifying and joining columns with the same name and data type. It is a valuable tool for associating related data and performing inner join operations within your data model.

36.ROW

Syntax:

ROW(<Column1>, <Value1>, [<Column2>, <Value2>, ...])

- `<Column1>`, `<Column2>`, ...: Columns to be included in the row.

- `<Value1>`, `<Value2>`, ...: Values to be assigned to the corresponding columns.

Description:

The **ROW** function in Power BI DAX is used to create a single-row table with specified columns and values. It allows you to define a custom row with specific data, which can be used in calculations, transformations, or as input to other DAX functions.

Example:

Suppose you want to create a custom row representing a new product with values for "ProductID," "ProductName," and "Price." You can use the ROW function as follows:

DAX Formula:

NewProduct = ROW(

   "ProductID", 101,

   "ProductName", "Widget",

   "Price", 19.99

)

Result: The "NewProduct" table will contain a single row with columns "ProductID," "ProductName," and "Price" and their respective values: 101, "Widget," and 19.99.

Tips:

- Use the **ROW** function when you need to create custom rows with specific column-value pairs. It is helpful for defining ad-hoc data within DAX expressions.

- Specify one or more pairs of `<Column>` and `<Value>` parameters within the **ROW** function to create the desired row structure.

- The resulting table from the **ROW** function contains a single row, and the columns and values specified in the function call.

- You can use the custom row created by **ROW** in calculations, table transformations, or as input to other DAX functions, allowing you to build dynamic and customized data structures.

- While **ROW** creates a single-row table, you can combine it with other DAX functions and operators to create more complex tables and perform various data modeling tasks.

- Remember that the column names and data types specified in the **ROW** function should match your data model's structure or the context in which the custom row will be used.

The **ROW** function provides flexibility in creating custom rows of data within Power BI DAX expressions. It is particularly useful when you need to define temporary or ad-hoc data for calculations and transformations.

37.SELECTCOLUMNS

Syntax:

SELECTCOLUMNS(

    table,

    [column1], expression1,

    [column2], expression2, ...

)

- `table`: The table or table expression to retrieve columns from.

- `[column1], [column2], ...`: Optional. Names of the new columns to create.

- `expression1, expression2, ...`: Expressions used to calculate values for the new columns.

Description:

The **SELECTCOLUMNS** function in Power BI DAX is used to create a new table by selecting specific columns from an existing table and optionally creating new columns based on expressions. It allows you to reshape data and calculate new values for analysis and reporting.

Example:

Suppose you have a table called "Sales" with columns "ProductID," "Quantity," and "Price," and you want to create a new table that includes the "ProductID," "TotalSales," and "DiscountedPrice" columns. You can use the **SELECTCOLUMNS** function as follows:

DAX Formula:

```
SalesSummary = SELECTCOLUMNS(
    'Sales',
    "ProductID", 'Sales'[ProductID],
    "TotalSales", 'Sales'[Quantity] * 'Sales'[Price],
    "DiscountedPrice", 'Sales'[Price] * 0.9  // Apply a 10% discount
)
```

Result: The "SalesSummary" table will include the "ProductID," "TotalSales," and "DiscountedPrice" columns, where "TotalSales" is calculated as the product of "Quantity" and "Price," and "DiscountedPrice" is calculated with a 10% discount applied to the original price.

Tips:

- Use the **SELECTCOLUMNS** function when you need to create a new table with specific columns from an existing table and optionally calculate values for new columns. It is useful for data reshaping and customization.

- Specify the source `table` from which you want to select columns.

- Use `[column]` and `expression` pairs to define the columns you want in the resulting table. You can create new columns by providing expressions that calculate values based on the source table's columns.

- The result of the **SELECTCOLUMNS** function is a new table with the specified columns and calculated values. It retains the column names provided in the function call.

- You can use **SELECTCOLUMNS** to create summary tables, calculated columns, or tables for specific analysis tasks.

- The expressions provided for calculating new column values can involve mathematical operations, functions, or other DAX expressions to manipulate the data as needed.

- Be mindful of column names and data types in the resulting table to ensure compatibility with your data model and intended use.

The **SELECTCOLUMNS** function is a versatile tool in Power BI DAX for selecting and transforming columns, allowing you to create customized tables tailored to your analysis and reporting needs.

38. UNION

Syntax:

UNION(Table1, Table2, [Table3], ...)

- `Table1`, `Table2`, `[Table3]`, ...: Tables or table expressions to combine into a single table.

Description:

The **UNION** function in Power BI DAX is used to combine multiple tables or table expressions into a single table by stacking their rows on top of each other. It is a way to append data vertically, creating a unified dataset.

Example:

Suppose you have two tables, "SalesQ1" and "SalesQ2," with the same column structure (e.g., "ProductID," "Quantity," "Price"). If you want to create a single table containing all sales data for both quarters, you can use the **UNION** function as follows:

DAX Formula:

CombinedSales = UNION('SalesQ1', 'SalesQ2')

Result: The "CombinedSales" table will contain all the rows from both "SalesQ1" and "SalesQ2," effectively merging the sales data for both quarters into one table.

Tips:

- Use the **UNION** function when you need to append rows from multiple tables into a single table. It is helpful for consolidating data from different sources or time periods.

- Specify one or more tables or table expressions as arguments to the **UNION** function. You can combine two or more tables in a single call.

- All tables provided to **UNION** should have the same column structure, including column names and data types. The function stacks rows on top of each other based on column structure.

- The resulting table from **UNION** includes all rows from the input tables, maintaining their original column names and data types.

- **UNION** is commonly used when you have similar data structures across multiple tables and want to create a unified dataset for analysis, reporting, or visualization.

- Be cautious when using **UNION** with large datasets, as it can significantly increase the size of your data model.

- Consider using **UNION** in conjunction with other DAX functions and filters to control the data you want to combine from different tables.

The **UNION** function simplifies the process of combining data from multiple sources or time periods into a single table, making it easier to perform analysis and create consolidated reports within Power BI.

CHAPTER V
Logical Functions

39.ALLEXCEPT

Syntax:

ALLEXCEPT(Table, [TableName], [ColumnName1], [ColumnName2], ...)

- `Table`: The table to which the filter context is applied.

- `[TableName]`: Optional. The name of the table from which all filters should be removed, except for the specified columns.

- `[ColumnName1], [ColumnName2], ...`: Optional. Columns for which filter context should be retained.

Description:

The **ALLEXCEPT** function in Power BI DAX is used to modify the filter context within a table or table expression by removing all filters except for the ones specified. It allows you to control which columns' filters are preserved while removing others, providing flexibility in data analysis.

Example:

Suppose you have a table called "Sales" with columns "ProductID," "Region," "Date," and "SalesAmount." If you want to calculate the total sales amount for all products but retain the filter context for the "Region" column, you can use the **ALLEXCEPT** function as follows:

DAX Formula:

TotalSales = CALCULATE(SUM('Sales'[SalesAmount]), ALLEXCEPT('Sales', 'Sales'[Region]))

Result: The "TotalSales" calculation will sum the "SalesAmount" column for all products but will retain the filter context for the "Region" column, allowing you to analyze sales within the selected region while ignoring filters on other columns.

Tips:

- Use the **ALLEXCEPT** function when you need to control the filter context within a DAX calculation or expression. It is particularly useful for scenarios where you want to retain specific filters while removing others.

- Specify the `Table` to which the filter context should be applied.

- Optionally, you can specify `[TableName]` to indicate the table from which all filters should be removed, except for the columns you want to retain. If `[TableName]` is not provided, the filter context is applied to the current table.

- Include `[ColumnName1], [ColumnName2], ...` to specify which columns' filters should be retained in the context. Filters on other columns will be removed.

- The result of the **ALLEXCEPT** function is a modified filter context for the specified table, where filters on the specified columns are preserved, and all other filters are removed.

- You can use **ALLEXCEPT** in combination with other DAX functions to perform calculations and aggregations while controlling the scope of filter context.

- Be mindful of the columns and tables you specify in the function to ensure that the filter context behaves as intended for your analysis.

The **ALLEXCEPT** function is a valuable tool in Power BI DAX for managing and controlling filter context within calculations, allowing for more precise and targeted data analysis and reporting.

40.ALLSELECTEDVALUES

Syntax:

ALLSELECTEDVALUES(Column, [AlternateResult])

- `Column`: The column for which you want to retrieve the unique value, considering all selected rows in the current filter context.

- `[AlternateResult]`: Optional. The value to return if there is more than one unique value in the specified column within the current filter context. If not provided, an error is returned when multiple values exist.

Description:

The **ALLSELECTEDVALUES** function in Power BI DAX is used to retrieve a unique value from a column, considering all selected rows within the current filter context. It is particularly useful when you want to ensure that only a single value is selected or when you need to extract a value based on the filter context.

Example:

Suppose you have a table called "Sales" with columns "ProductID," "Region," "Date," and "SalesAmount." If you want to retrieve the unique "Region" value selected in the current filter context, you can use the **ALLSELECTEDVALUES** function as follows:

DAX Formula:

SelectedRegion = ALLSELECTEDVALUES('Sales'[Region])

Result: The "SelectedRegion" will contain the unique "Region" value selected in the current filter context. If multiple regions are selected, an error will occur unless you provide an `[AlternateResult]` value.

Tips:

- Use the **ALLSELECTEDVALUES** function when you need to retrieve a unique value from a column based on the current filter context. It is helpful for scenarios where you want to ensure a single value is selected or need to extract a value from a filtered dataset.

- Specify the `Column` for which you want to retrieve the unique value. The function considers all selected rows in the current filter context to determine the value.

- Optionally, provide an `[AlternateResult]` value to handle cases where there is more than one unique value in the specified column within the filter context. Without an alternate result, an error will be returned for multiple values.

- The result of the **ALLSELECTEDVALUES** function is a single value from the specified column, based on the filter context. If the filter context contains multiple rows with different values, you must provide an `[AlternateResult]` or expect an error.

- **ALLSELECTEDVALUES** is commonly used in calculations and measures to extract specific values, such as selected dimensions or attributes, for further analysis or visualization.

- Be cautious when using this function in scenarios where multiple values might exist within the filter context, and ensure you handle such cases with appropriate alternate results or error handling.

The **ALLSELECTEDVALUES** function provides a straightforward way to extract a single unique value from a column within the current filter context, making it valuable for various analytical and reporting scenarios in Power BI.

41.AND

Syntax:

AND(condition1, condition2, ...)

- `condition1`, `condition2`, ...: Boolean expressions or conditions that you want to evaluate as true or false.

Description:

The **AND** function in Power BI DAX is used to check if multiple conditions or Boolean expressions are all true. It returns TRUE if all the specified conditions are true; otherwise, it returns FALSE. It's often used for complex filtering and logic in calculations and measures.

Example:

Suppose you have a table of sales data with columns "Region," "Product," and "SalesAmount." You want to create a measure that checks if both the sales amount is greater than 1000 and the region is "North." You can use the AND function as follows:

DAX Formula:

HighSalesInNorth = IF(AND('Sales'[SalesAmount] > 1000, 'Sales'[Region] = "North"), TRUE(), FALSE())

Result: The "HighSalesInNorth" measure will return TRUE when both conditions, sales amount > 1000 and region = "North," are met for the current filter context; otherwise, it will return FALSE.

Tips:

- Use the **AND** function when you need to evaluate multiple conditions and require all of them to be true to return a TRUE result. It is commonly used for complex filtering and logical calculations.

- Specify one or more `condition` arguments, where each condition is a Boolean expression or a logical test.

- **AND** returns TRUE only if all the conditions are TRUE. If any of the conditions is FALSE, it returns FALSE.

- You can nest **AND** functions to create more complex conditions by combining multiple sets of conditions.

- The result of the **AND** function is a Boolean value, either TRUE or FALSE, based on the evaluation of the specified conditions.

- **AND** can be used in various scenarios, such as creating calculated columns, measures, or calculated tables, where you need to check multiple criteria simultaneously.

- Be cautious when using **AND** with complex conditions to ensure that the logic aligns with your analysis requirements. Verify that each condition is correctly evaluated.

The **AND** function is a fundamental tool in Power BI DAX for evaluating multiple conditions and creating more advanced logic in your data models and calculations.

42.COALESCE

Syntax:

COALESCE(value1, value2, ...)

- `value1`, `value2`, ...: Values or expressions to evaluate. The function returns the first non-blank value found from left to right.

Description:

The **COALESCE** function in Power BI DAX is used to return the first non-blank value from a list of values or expressions. It is particularly useful when dealing with multiple columns or measures, and you want to find the first value that is not blank or null.

Example:

Suppose you have a table of employee data with columns "FirstName," "MiddleName," and "LastName." You want to create a calculated column that contains the first non-blank name (considering both first and middle names). You can use the COALESCE function as follows:

DAX Formula:

FullName = COALESCE('Employees'[FirstName], 'Employees'[MiddleName], 'Employees'[LastName])

Result: The "FullName" calculated column will contain the first non-blank name found from left to right, considering "FirstName," "MiddleName," and "LastName" columns.

Tips:

- Use the **COALESCE** function when you want to find the first non-blank or non-null value from a list of values or expressions. It is valuable for consolidating information from multiple sources or columns.

- Specify multiple `value` arguments to evaluate. The function checks these values from left to right and returns the first non-blank value it encounters.

- **COALESCE** returns the first non-blank value, and if all values are blank or null, it returns a blank result.

- You can use **COALESCE** with a combination of columns, measures, or expressions, making it versatile for handling different data types.

- Be cautious when using **COALESCE** with large datasets or expressions, as it evaluates each argument in sequence, and evaluating complex expressions may impact performance.

- The result of the **COALESCE** function is a single value or a blank result, depending on the evaluation of the specified values.

The **COALESCE** function simplifies the process of finding the first non-blank value from a list of options, making it a useful tool for data consolidation and data modeling in Power BI.

43. IF

Syntax:

IF(condition, value_if_true, value_if_false)

- `condition`: A Boolean expression or a test that you want to evaluate.

- `value_if_true`: The value or expression to return if the `condition` is true.

- `value_if_false`: The value or expression to return if the `condition` is false.

Description:

The **IF** function in Power BI DAX is used for conditional logic. It evaluates a specified condition and returns one of two possible results based on whether the condition is true or false. This function is essential for creating calculated columns and measures that involve decision-making based on data conditions.

Example:

Suppose you have a table of sales data with a "SalesAmount" column, and you want to create a calculated column that categorizes sales as "High" if the sales amount is greater than 1000 and "Low" otherwise. You can use the **IF** function as follows:

DAX Formula:

SalesCategory = IF('Sales'[SalesAmount] > 1000, "High", "Low")

Result: The "SalesCategory" calculated column will contain the category "High" for sales amounts greater than 1000 and "Low" for sales amounts less than or equal to 1000.

Tips:

- Use the **IF** function when you need to apply conditional logic in your calculations or measures. It allows you to make decisions based on data conditions.

- Specify a `condition` that evaluates to either true or false. If the condition is true, the function returns `value_if_true`; if false, it returns `value_if_false`.

- You can use any valid DAX expression as `value_if_true` and `value_if_false`. These can be constants, column references, or more complex calculations.

- **IF** can be nested to create more complex conditional logic. For example, you can have multiple levels of conditions based on your analysis requirements.

- The result of the **IF** function is the value specified in either `value_if_true` or `value_if_false`, depending on the evaluation of the `condition`.

- Carefully plan your conditions and outcomes to ensure the logic aligns with your analysis goals.

The **IF** function is a fundamental tool in Power BI DAX for introducing conditional logic into your data models. It helps you categorize, filter, and calculate values based on specific criteria, enabling more advanced and customized data analysis and reporting.

44.IFBLANK

Syntax:

IFBLANK(expression, [alternate_result])

- `expression`: The expression or value you want to evaluate for blank or null values.

- `[alternate_result]`: Optional. The value to return if the `expression` is blank or null. If not provided, a blank result is returned.

Description:

The **IFBLANK** function in Power BI DAX is used to check if a given expression or value is blank or null. It returns the `expression` itself if it's not blank or null; otherwise, it returns an optional `[alternate_result]`. This function is helpful for handling missing or null values in calculations and measures.

Example:

Suppose you have a table with sales data and a column "DiscountAmount," and you want to create a calculated column that displays the discount amount if it's available, or a message if it's blank. You can use the **IFBLANK** function as follows:

DAX Formula:

DiscountMessage = IFBLANK('Sales'[DiscountAmount], "No Discount Available")

Result: The "DiscountMessage" calculated column will display the discount amount if it's not blank; otherwise, it will show the message "No Discount Available."

Tips:

- Use the **IFBLANK** function when you want to handle blank or null values in your calculations or measures. It allows you to provide an alternate result when the original expression is blank.

- Specify the `expression` you want to evaluate for blank or null values. If the expression is not blank, it is returned as is; otherwise, an optional `[alternate_result]` is used.

- The `[alternate_result]` can be any valid DAX expression, such as a constant value, column reference, or more complex calculation. It is returned when the `expression` is blank or null.

- You can use **IFBLANK** in various scenarios, such as displaying informative messages, substituting missing values, or controlling the behavior of your calculations.

- Be mindful of the potential impact of handling blank or null values on your analysis. Ensure that the alternate result provided aligns with your data modeling and reporting goals.

The **IFBLANK** function is a valuable tool in Power BI DAX for addressing missing or null values in your data models. It allows you to gracefully handle such cases by providing customized responses or values based on your analysis requirements.

45.IFERROR

Syntax:

IFERROR(expression, [value_if_error])

- `expression`: The expression or value you want to evaluate for errors.

- `[value_if_error]`: Optional. The value to return if the `expression` results in an error. If not provided, a blank result is returned.

Description:

The **IFERROR** function in Power BI DAX is used to check if a given expression or value results in an error. It returns the `expression` itself if it does not produce an error; otherwise, it returns an optional `[value_if_error]`. This function is valuable for handling errors in calculations and measures.

Example:

Suppose you have a table with sales data, and you want to create a calculated column that calculates the profit margin by dividing "Profit" by "Revenue." However, there may be cases where "Revenue" is zero, resulting in a division error. You can use the IFERROR function to handle this scenario:

DAX Formula:

ProfitMargin = IFERROR('Sales'[Profit] / 'Sales'[Revenue], 0)

Result: The "ProfitMargin" calculated column will contain the calculated profit margin, but if a division error occurs (e.g., when "Revenue" is zero), it will return 0 instead of an error.

Tips:

- Use the **IFERROR** function when you want to handle errors that may occur during calculations. It allows you to provide an alternate result when the original expression results in an error.

- Specify the `expression` you want to evaluate for errors. If the expression does not produce an error, it is returned as is; otherwise, an optional `[value_if_error]` is used.

- The `[value_if_error]` can be any valid DAX expression, such as a constant value, column reference, or more complex calculation. It is returned when the `expression` results in an error.

- **IFERROR** is particularly useful for scenarios involving division by zero, where you want to replace errors with a meaningful value.

- Be mindful of the types of errors that may occur in your calculations and ensure that the `[value_if_error]` provided aligns with your data modeling and reporting goals.

The **IFERROR** function is a valuable tool in Power BI DAX for handling errors that may arise during calculations. It enables you to gracefully manage errors by providing customized responses or values based on your analysis requirements.

46.IFNA

Syntax:

IFNA(value, value_if_na)

- `value`: The value or expression to evaluate.

- `value_if_na`: The value to return if `value` is a #N/A error.

Description:

The **IFNA** function in Power BI DAX is used to check if a given value or expression results in a #N/A error (commonly used to represent missing data). It returns the `value` itself if it's not a #N/A error; otherwise, it returns an optional `value_if_na`. This function is valuable for handling missing or not available (NA) data in calculations and measures.

Example:

Suppose you have a table with product data, and you want to create a calculated column that calculates the price-to-sales ratio by dividing "Price" by "Sales." If there is missing sales data (represented as #N/A), you want to display a message. You can use the IFNA function as follows:

DAX Formula:

PriceToSalesRatio = IFNA('Products'[Price] / 'Products'[Sales], "Sales Data Not Available")

Result: The "PriceToSalesRatio" calculated column will contain the calculated ratio, but if sales data is missing (resulting in a #N/A error), it will display the message "Sales Data Not Available."

Tips:

- Use the **IFNA** function when you want to handle #N/A errors, often used to represent missing or not available data. It allows you to provide an alternate result when the original value is #N/A.

- Specify the `value` you want to evaluate for #N/A errors. If the value is not #N/A, it is returned as is; otherwise, an optional `value_if_na` is used.

- The `value_if_na` can be any valid DAX expression, such as a constant value, column reference, or more complex calculation. It is returned when the `value` is #N/A.

- **IFNA** is particularly useful for scenarios where you want to handle missing or not available data gracefully, providing informative messages or alternate values.

- Be aware of the types of data representations used for missing data in your dataset (such as #N/A) and ensure that the `value_if_na` provided aligns with your data modeling and reporting goals.

The **IFNA** function is a valuable tool in Power BI DAX for managing #N/A errors and handling missing or not available data in your data models. It allows you to customize the response or value when dealing with such data representations.

47.NOT

Syntax:

NOT(logical_expression)

- `logical_expression`: A logical expression or value to negate (reverse).

Description:

The **NOT** function in Power BI DAX is used to reverse or negate a logical expression. It evaluates the `logical_expression` and returns the opposite of its result. If the `logical_expression` is true, **NOT** returns false, and if the `logical_expression` is false, **NOT** returns true. This function is valuable for making logical comparisons and filtering data based on conditions.

Example:

Suppose you have a table with employee data, and you want to create a measure that calculates the number of employees who are not on vacation. You can use the **NOT** function to reverse the logical expression:

DAX Formula:

EmployeesNotOnVacation = CALCULATE(COUNT('Employees'[EmployeeID]), NOT('Employees'[OnVacation] = TRUE))

Result: The "EmployeesNotOnVacation" measure will return the count of employees who are not on vacation by reversing the logical expression "OnVacation = TRUE."

Tips:

- Use the **NOT** function when you need to reverse the logical result of a condition or expression. It is often used in conjunction with other logical functions to create complex filtering conditions.

- Provide a `logical_expression` that you want to negate. If the expression is true, **NOT** returns false, and if the expression is false, **NOT** returns true.

- **NOT** can be useful for creating filters, defining custom conditions, or changing the behavior of calculations based on logical criteria.

- Be cautious when using **NOT** in complex DAX calculations, as it can affect the overall logic and results. Ensure that the negation aligns with your analytical goals.

The **NOT** function is a fundamental tool in Power BI DAX for reversing logical expressions, allowing you to create flexible and customized data analysis and filtering conditions based on your specific requirements.

48.NOTBLANK

Syntax:

NOTBLANK(expression)

- `expression`: The expression or column to check for non-blank values.

Description:

The **NOTBLANK** function in Power BI DAX is used to determine if a given expression or column contains non-blank values. It returns true if at least one non-blank value is found in the expression; otherwise, it returns false. This function is valuable for filtering or counting data based on the presence of non-blank values.

Example:

Suppose you have a table with customer data, and you want to create a measure that counts the number of customers who have provided their email addresses. You can use the **NOTBLANK** function as follows:

DAX Formula:

CustomersWithEmail = CALCULATE(COUNT('Customers'[CustomerID]), NOTBLANK('Customers'[Email]))

Result: The "CustomersWithEmail" measure will return the count of customers who have provided their email addresses.

Tips:

- Use the **NOTBLANK** function when you need to check if a specific expression or column contains non-blank values. It is often used for filtering or counting data based on the presence of data in a particular column.

- Specify the `expression` you want to evaluate for non-blank values. If at least one non-blank value is found, **NOTBLANK** returns true; otherwise, it returns false.

- **NOTBLANK** is particularly useful for scenarios where you want to identify or count records with data in specific columns.

- Be mindful of the data quality and completeness when using **NOTBLANK**, as it relies on the presence of non-blank values in the specified expression.

The **NOTBLANK** function is a valuable tool in Power BI DAX for assessing the presence of non-blank data, enabling you to create dynamic calculations and measures based on data completeness or specific column values in your analysis.

49.OR

Syntax:

OR(<logical1>, <logical2>, ...)

- `<logical1>, <logical2>, ...`: One or more logical expressions or values to test.

Description:

The **OR** function in Power BI DAX is used to perform logical OR operations on one or more expressions or values. It checks if at least one of the provided expressions is true and returns true if any of them evaluates to true; otherwise, it returns false. This function is valuable for creating complex conditions and filtering data based on multiple logical criteria.

Example:

Suppose you have a table with sales data, and you want to create a measure that counts the number of products that have either high sales or a high profit margin. You can use the OR function as follows:

DAX Formula:

HighSalesOrMarginProducts = CALCULATE(COUNT('Products'[ProductID]),
OR('Products'[Sales] > 1000, 'Products'[ProfitMargin] > 0.2))

Result: The "HighSalesOrMarginProducts" measure will return the count of products that meet either of the specified conditions (sales > 1000 or profit margin > 20%).

Tips:

- Use the **OR** function when you need to perform logical OR operations on multiple expressions or values. It allows you to create complex conditions by combining multiple criteria.

- Provide one or more `<logical>` expressions that you want to test. If at least one of them is true, **OR** returns true; otherwise, it returns false.

- **OR** is valuable for defining filtering conditions, calculating results based on multiple criteria, and creating dynamic measures.

- Be cautious when using **OR** in complex DAX calculations, as it affects the overall logic and results. Ensure that the combination of logical expressions aligns with your analytical goals.

The **OR** function is a versatile tool in Power BI DAX for performing logical OR operations, enabling you to create flexible and customized data analysis and filtering conditions based on multiple criteria.

50.SWITCH

Syntax:

SWITCH(expression, value1, result1, value2, result2, ..., [default_result])

- `expression`: The expression to evaluate.

- `value1, value2, ...`: The values to compare with the `expression`.

- `result1, result2, ...`: The results to return if the corresponding `value` matches the `expression`.

- `[default_result]` (optional): The result to return if none of the `value` expressions match the `expression`.

Description:

The **SWITCH** function in Power BI DAX is used to perform multiple conditional checks in a concise and structured way. It evaluates the `expression` and compares it to a series of `value` expressions. If a match is found, it returns the corresponding `result`. If no matches are found, it returns the optional `[default_result]` if specified; otherwise, it returns a blank.

Example:

Suppose you have a table with sales data, and you want to create a calculated column that categorizes products based on their sales amounts. You can use the SWITCH function as follows:

DAX Formula:

```
ProductCategory =
SWITCH(
    TRUE(),
    'Products'[Sales] > 1000, "High Sales",
    'Products'[Sales] > 500, "Moderate Sales",
    'Products'[Sales] > 100, "Low Sales",
    "Very Low Sales"
)
```

Result: The "ProductCategory" calculated column will categorize products based on their sales amounts, with different categories like "High Sales," "Moderate Sales," "Low Sales," or "Very Low Sales."

Tips:

- Use the **SWITCH** function when you need to perform multiple conditional checks and return different results based on those checks. It provides a structured and efficient way to handle complex conditions.

- Start with the `expression` to evaluate. It can be any valid DAX expression or column.

- Specify pairs of `value` and `result` expressions, which are evaluated in sequence. The first `value` that matches the `expression` triggers the corresponding `result`.

- You can include an optional `[default_result]` to handle cases where none of the `value` expressions match the `expression`.

- **SWITCH** is particularly useful when dealing with mutually exclusive conditions or categorizing data into multiple categories.

The **SWITCH** function simplifies conditional logic in Power BI DAX, allowing you to efficiently handle multiple conditions and return customized results based on those conditions.

CHAPTER VI
Date and Time Functions

51.CALENDAR

Syntax:

CALENDAR(start_date, end_date)

- `start_date`: The start date for the calendar.

- `end_date`: The end date for the calendar.

Description:

The **CALENDAR** function in Power BI DAX is used to generate a table with a single column that contains a continuous range of dates from the `start_date` to the `end_date`. This function is valuable for creating date tables that can be used for time-based analysis, such as calculating sales trends or aggregating data by date.

Example:

Suppose you want to create a date table for analyzing sales data for the year 2023. You can use the **CALENDAR** function as follows:

DAX Formula:

CalendarTable = CALENDAR(DATE(2023, 1, 1), DATE(2023, 12, 31))

Result: The "CalendarTable" will contain a single column with dates from January 1, 2023, to December 31, 2023.

Tips:

- Use the **CALENDAR** function to generate date tables that are essential for time-based analysis and calculations in Power BI.

- Specify the `start_date` and `end_date` to define the date range you want in the table.

- Date tables created with **CALENDAR** can be used for various time-based calculations, including year-to-date totals, month-over-month comparisons, and more.

- Be mindful of the date format and data type when working with date tables, as they impact date-related calculations.

The **CALENDAR** function simplifies the process of creating date tables in Power BI, providing a foundation for analyzing and visualizing data over time.

52. DATE

Syntax:

DATE(year, month, day)

- `year`: An integer representing the year.

- `month`: An integer representing the month (1 to 12).

- `day`: An integer representing the day of the month (1 to 31).

Description:

The **DATE** function in Power BI DAX is used to create a date value based on the provided `year`, `month`, and `day`. It combines these components to generate a date that can be used for various date-related calculations and analysis.

Example:

Suppose you want to create a calculated column in a table that represents the date "October 15, 2023." You can use the DATE function as follows:

DAX Formula:

DateColumn = DATE(2023, 10, 15)

Result: The "DateColumn" will contain the date "October 15, 2023."

Tips:

- Use the **DATE** function when you need to create date values dynamically based on separate components (year, month, day).

- Ensure that the provided `year`, `month`, and `day` are valid integers and within their respective ranges (e.g., month should be between 1 and 12).

- Date values created with **DATE** can be used for date-based calculations, such as calculating the difference between dates or filtering data within a specific date range.

- Be aware of the date format and data type when working with date values in Power BI, as they impact date-related calculations and formatting.

The **DATE** function is a fundamental tool for generating date values in Power BI, enabling you to work with date data effectively and perform various date-related analyses.

53. DATEADD

Syntax:

DATEADD(start_date, number_of_intervals, interval)

- `start_date`: The initial date to which intervals are added or subtracted.

- `number_of_intervals`: The number of intervals to add or subtract.

- `interval`: A string specifying the type of interval to use for calculations (e.g., "day," "month," "year").

Description:

The **DATEADD** function in Power BI DAX is used to perform date calculations by adding or subtracting a specified number of intervals (such as days, months, or years) to a given `start date`. This function is valuable for shifting dates in time-based analysis, creating date ranges, or performing date-based comparisons.

Example:

Suppose you have a date column and you want to create a new column that represents the date 30 days after the original date. You can use the DATEADD function as follows:

DAX Formula:

NewDate = DATEADD('Sales'[OrderDate], 30, DAY)

Result: The "NewDate" column will contain dates that are 30 days after the corresponding dates in the "OrderDate" column.

Tips:

- Use the **DATEADD** function when you need to perform date calculations by adding or subtracting intervals to or from a given date.

- Specify the `start_date` as the base date for calculations, `number_of_intervals` to determine how many intervals to add or subtract, and `interval` to define the type of interval (e.g., "day," "month," "year").

- The `interval` parameter accepts a variety of interval types, allowing you to perform precise date manipulations.

- Be aware of the data types and formatting of date columns when working with **DATEADD** to ensure accurate calculations.

The **DATEADD** function is a versatile tool for performing date calculations in Power BI, enabling you to work with dates dynamically and perform various time-based analyses.

54.DATEDIFF

Syntax:

DATEDIFF(start_date, end_date, interval)

- `start_date`: The start date of the date range.

- `end_date`: The end date of the date range.

- `interval`: A string specifying the type of interval for the calculation (e.g., "day," "month," "quarter," "year").

Description:

The **DATEDIFF** function in Power BI DAX calculates the difference between two dates in terms of a specified interval. It provides flexibility in measuring time gaps between dates, making it valuable for various date-based analyses, such as calculating age, duration, or time between events.

Example:

Suppose you have a dataset with two date columns: "StartDate" and "EndDate." You want to calculate the duration (in days) between these two dates. You can use the DATEDIFF function as follows:

DAX Formula:

DurationInDays = DATEDIFF([StartDate], [EndDate], DAY)

Result: The "DurationInDays" column will contain the number of days between the "StartDate" and "EndDate" for each row in the dataset.

Tips:

- Utilize the **DATEDIFF** function when you need to calculate the difference between two dates in terms of a specified interval.

- Specify the `start_date` and `end_date` to define the date range for the calculation and use the `interval` parameter to determine the type of interval (e.g., "day," "month," "quarter," "year").

- The `interval` parameter offers various options for interval types, allowing you to measure time differences precisely.

- Pay attention to the data types and formats of date columns to ensure accurate calculations with **DATEDIFF.**

The **DATEDIFF** function is a powerful tool for conducting date-based calculations in Power BI, enabling you to analyze time gaps and durations effectively in your data.

55.DATESMTD

Syntax:

DATESMTD(start_date)

- `start_date`: A date expression representing the date within the month for which you want to calculate the month-to-date period.

Description:

The **DATESMTD** function in Power BI DAX is used to calculate the month-to-date (MTD) period ending on a specified date. It is commonly used to aggregate data for the current month up to a specific date, making it useful for tracking monthly progress and performing MTD comparisons.

Example:

Suppose you have a sales dataset with a date column named "OrderDate," and you want to calculate the total sales for the month-to-date period ending on September 15, 2023. You can use the **DATESMTD** function as follows:

DAX Formula:

MTD_Sales = CALCULATE(SUM('Sales'[SalesAmount]), DATESMTD('Calendar'[Date], "2023-09-15"))

Result: The "MTD_Sales" measure will give you the total sales for the month of September 2023 up to September 15, 2023.

Tips:

- Use the **DATESMTD** function when you need to calculate values for the month-to-date period ending on a specific date.

- Provide a valid date expression as the `start_date` parameter, which represents the date within the desired month.

- **DATESMTD** is often used in combination with other aggregation functions, such as **SUM**, to perform calculations on MTD data.

- Be mindful of the date format and data type to ensure accurate calculations with **DATESMTD.**

The **DATESMTD** function is a valuable tool for tracking and analyzing month-to-date data in Power BI, allowing you to gain insights into your data's monthly performance.

56.DATESQTD

Syntax:

DATESQTD(start_date)

- `start_date`: A date expression representing the date within the quarter for which you want to calculate the quarter-to-date period.

Description:

The **DATESQTD** function in Power BI DAX is used to calculate the quarter-to-date (QTD) period ending on a specified date. It allows you to aggregate data for the current quarter up to a specific date, making it useful for tracking quarterly progress and performing QTD comparisons.

Example:

Suppose you have a financial dataset with a date column named "TransactionDate," and you want to calculate the total revenue for the quarter-to-date period ending on September 15, 2023. You can use the **DATESQTD** function as follows:

DAX Formula:

QTD_Revenue = CALCULATE(SUM('FinancialData'[Revenue]),
DATESQTD('Calendar'[Date], "2023-09-15"))

Result: The "QTD_Revenue" measure will provide the total revenue for the third quarter of 2023 up to September 15, 2023.

Tips:

- Utilize the **DATESQTD** function when you need to calculate values for the quarter-to-date period ending on a specific date.

- Provide a valid date expression as the `start_date` parameter, which represents the date within the desired quarter.

- **DATESQTD** is often used in combination with other aggregation functions, such as **SUM**, to perform calculations on QTD data.

- Ensure that the date format and data type are consistent to achieve accurate calculations with **DATESQTD.**

The **DATESQTD** function is a valuable tool for analyzing and monitoring quarter-to-date data in Power BI, enabling you to assess your data's quarterly performance effectively.

57.DATESYTD

Syntax:

DATESYTD(start_date, year_end_date)

- `start_date`: A date expression representing the date within the year for which you want to calculate the year-to-date period.

- `year_end_date`: (Optional) A date expression specifying the end date of the fiscal year. If not provided, the calendar year end date (December 31st) is used by default.

Description:

The **DATESYTD** function in Power BI DAX is used to calculate the year-to-date (YTD) period ending on a specified date. It allows you to aggregate data for the current year up to a specific date, making it useful for tracking annual progress and performing YTD comparisons. You can optionally specify a fiscal year end date to align the calculation with your organization's fiscal year.

Example:

Suppose you have a financial dataset with a date column named "TransactionDate," and you want to calculate the total revenue for the year-to-date period ending on September 15, 2023, considering a fiscal year ending on June 30th. You can use the **DATESYTD** function as follows:

DAX Formula:

YTD_Revenue = CALCULATE(SUM('FinancialData'[Revenue]),
DATESYTD('Calendar'[Date], "2023-09-15", "2023-06-30"))

Result: The "YTD_Revenue" measure will provide the total revenue for the fiscal year 2023 up to September 15, 2023, considering a fiscal year end date of June 30th.

KIET HUYNH

Tips:

- Use the **DATESYTD** function when you need to calculate values for the year-to-date period ending on a specific date.

- Provide a valid date expression as the `start_date` parameter, which represents the date within the desired year.

- You can optionally specify a `year_end_date` parameter to align the calculation with your organization's fiscal year. If omitted, the calendar year end date (December 31st) is used.

- **DATESYTD** is often used in combination with other aggregation functions, such as **SUM**, to perform calculations on YTD data.

- Ensure that the date format and data type are consistent for accurate calculations with **DATESYTD.**

The **DATESYTD** function is a valuable tool for analyzing and monitoring year-to-date data in Power BI, allowing you to assess your data's annual performance effectively, especially when considering custom fiscal year endings.

58.DAY

Syntax:

DAY(date)

- `date`: A date expression from which you want to extract the day component.

Description:

The **DAY** function in Power BI DAX is used to extract the day component (day of the month) from a given date. It returns an integer between 1 and 31, representing the day of the specified date.

Example:

Suppose you have a date column named "OrderDate" in your sales dataset, and you want to create a measure that calculates the total sales made on the 10th day of each month. You can use the **DAY** function as follows:

DAX Formula:

Sales_On_10th   =   CALCULATE(SUM('SalesData'[SalesAmount]), DAY('SalesData'[OrderDate]) = 10)

Result: The "Sales_On_10th" measure will provide the total sales amount for all orders made on the 10th day of each month.

Tips:

- Use the **DAY** function when you need to extract the day component from a date.

- The returned value will be an integer between 1 and 31.

- **DAY** is often used in combination with other functions or as a filter condition to perform date-related calculations.

- Ensure that your date column has the appropriate data type (Date/Time) for accurate results with the **DAY** function.

The **DAY** function is a useful tool for working with date data in Power BI, allowing you to extract specific date components for various analytical purposes.

59. EOMONTH

Syntax:

EOMONTH(start_date, months)

- `start_date`: A date expression representing the start date from which you want to calculate the end of the month.

- `months`: An integer representing the number of months to add or subtract from the start date. Positive values add months, and negative values subtract months.

Description:

The **EOMONTH** function in Power BI DAX is used to calculate the last day of the month relative to a specified date. It allows you to determine the end date of the month that is a certain number of months before or after a given date.

Example:

Suppose you have a sales dataset with a date column named "InvoiceDate," and you want to calculate the end of the month for each invoice's date. You can use the EOMONTH function as follows:

DAX Formula:

EndOfMonth = EOMONTH('SalesData'[InvoiceDate], 0)

Result: The "EndOfMonth" column will contain the last day of the month corresponding to each invoice date.

Tips:

- Use the **EOMONTH** function when you need to find the last day of a month relative to a given date.

- The `months` parameter allows you to specify how many months to add or subtract from the `start_date`. A value of 0 returns the end of the same month as the `start_date`.

- You can use **EOMONTH** in various date-related calculations, such as calculating monthly totals or aggregating data by month.

- Ensure that your date column has the appropriate data type (Date/Time) for accurate results with the **EOMONTH** function.

The **EOMONTH** function is a valuable tool for working with date data in Power BI, especially when you need to perform calculations that involve month-end dates or aggregations.

60. HOUR

Syntax:

HOUR(time)

- `time`: A time expression from which you want to extract the hour component.

Description:

The **HOUR** function in Power BI DAX is used to extract the hour component from a given time. It returns an integer between 0 and 23, representing the hour of the specified time.

Example:

Suppose you have a time column named "OrderTime" in your sales dataset, and you want to create a measure that calculates the total sales made during a specific hour of the day (e.g., between 3 PM and 4 PM). You can use the HOUR function as follows:

DAX Formula:

Sales_During_3PM_to_4PM = CALCULATE(SUM('SalesData'[SalesAmount]), HOUR('SalesData'[OrderTime]) = 15)

Result: The "Sales_During_3PM_to_4PM" measure will provide the total sales amount for all orders made between 3 PM and 4 PM.

Tips:

- Use the **HOUR** function when you need to extract the hour component from a time.

- The returned value will be an integer between 0 and 23, representing the hour of the specified time.

- **HOUR** is often used in combination with other functions or as a filter condition to perform time-related calculations.

- Ensure that your time column has the appropriate data type (Date/Time) for accurate results with the **HOUR** function.

The **HOUR** function is a valuable tool for working with time data in Power BI, allowing you to extract specific time components for various analytical purposes.

61.MINUTE

Syntax:

MINUTE(time)

- `time`: A time expression from which you want to extract the minute component.

Description:

The **MINUTE** function in Power BI DAX is used to extract the minute component from a given time. It returns an integer between 0 and 59, representing the minute of the specified time.

Example:

Suppose you have a time column named "StartTime" in your dataset that records the start time of events, and you want to calculate the average duration of these events in minutes. You can use the **MINUTE** function in combination with other functions as follows:

DAX Formula:

Average_Event_Duration_Minutes =
  AVERAGEX(
    Events,
    MINUTE(Events[EndTime] - Events[StartTime])
)

Result: The "Average_Event_Duration_Minutes" measure will provide the average duration of events in minutes.

Tips:

- Use the **MINUTE** function when you need to extract the minute component from a time.

- The returned value will be an integer between 0 and 59, representing the minute of the specified time.

- **MINUTE** is often used in combination with other date and time functions to perform time-related calculations, such as calculating durations, intervals, or aggregations by minute.

- Ensure that your time column has the appropriate data type (Date/Time) for accurate results with the **MINUTE** function.

The **MINUTE** function is a valuable tool for working with time data in Power BI, allowing you to extract specific time components for various analytical purposes.

62.MONTH

Syntax:

MONTH(date)

- `date`: A date expression from which you want to extract the month component.

Description:

The **MONTH** function in Power BI DAX is used to extract the month component from a given date. It returns an integer between 1 and 12, representing the month of the specified date.

Example:

Suppose you have a date column named "OrderDate" in your sales dataset, and you want to create a measure that calculates the total sales made in a specific month (e.g., January). You can use the **MONTH** function as follows:

DAX Formula:

Sales_In_January = CALCULATE(SUM('SalesData'[SalesAmount]), MONTH('SalesData'[OrderDate]) = 1)

Result: The "Sales_In_January" measure will provide the total sales amount for all orders made in January.

Tips:

- Use the **MONTH** function when you need to extract the month component from a date.

- The returned value will be an integer between 1 and 12, representing the month of the specified date.

- **MONTH** is often used in combination with other date and time functions to perform time-related calculations, such as aggregating data by month, quarter, or year.

- Ensure that your date column has the appropriate data type (Date) for accurate results with the **MONTH** function.

The **MONTH** function is a valuable tool for working with date data in Power BI, allowing you to extract specific date components for various analytical purposes.

63.NOW

Syntax:

NOW()

Description:

The **NOW** function in Power BI DAX returns the current date and time as a datetime value. This function does not require any arguments and provides a timestamp representing the current date and time when the formula is evaluated.

Example:

Suppose you want to create a measure that calculates the number of orders placed today in your sales dataset. You can use the **NOW** function in combination with other functions as follows:

DAX Formula:

Orders_Placed_Today =
    COUNTROWS(

```
FILTER(

    Sales,

    Sales[OrderDate] = TODAY()

    )

)
```

Result: The "Orders_Placed_Today" measure will provide the count of orders placed on the current date as per the system's clock.

Tips:

- Use the **NOW** function when you need to capture the current date and time within your DAX formula.

- The **NOW** function can be helpful for time-sensitive calculations and comparisons, such as determining how many records are associated with the current date or time.

- Remember that the result of the **NOW** function will change each time your Power BI report or data model is refreshed or recalculated, as it reflects the current system date and time.

- To work with the current date only (without the time component), you can use the **TODAY** function, which returns the current date as a date value.

The **NOW** function allows you to incorporate real-time date and time values into your Power BI calculations and is particularly useful for tracking events or data changes based on the current timestamp.

64.SAMEPERIODLASTMONTH

Syntax:

SAMEPERIODLASTMONTH(<Dates>)

Description:

The SAMEPERIODLASTMONTH function in Power BI DAX returns a table that contains all the dates from the previous month within the same time intelligence level as the input dates. This function is typically used for time-based calculations and comparisons where you want to retrieve data from the equivalent period in the previous month.

- `<Dates>`: This is the column or table of dates for which you want to find the equivalent period in the previous month.

Example:

Suppose you have a sales dataset with a column named "OrderDate" and you want to calculate the total sales for the same period (same number of days) in the previous month. You can use the **SAMEPERIODLASTMONTH** function as follows:

DAX Formula:

Total Sales Last Month =
    SUMX(
        FILTER(

```
    Sales,

    NOT(ISBLANK(Sales[SalesAmount]))

  ),

  Sales[SalesAmount]

)
```

Result: The "Total Sales Last Month" measure will provide the sum of sales amounts for the equivalent period in the previous month.

Tips:

- The **SAMEPERIODLASTMONTH** function is useful for creating month-over-month or year-over-year comparisons in your Power BI reports.

- Ensure that your date column is marked as a date table within your Power BI data model for this function to work correctly.

- You can customize the time intelligence level by changing the `<Dates>` argument. For example, you can use `[OrderDate].[Month]` to retrieve the equivalent month in the previous year.

- Be cautious when using this function with a date filter, as it may return unexpected results if not used correctly within your calculations.

The **SAMEPERIODLASTMONTH** function is a valuable tool for analyzing trends and comparing data between the current and previous months, enabling you to gain insights into your business's performance over time.

65.SAMEPERIODLASTQUARTER

Syntax:

SAMEPERIODLASTQUARTER(<Dates>)

Description:

The **SAMEPERIODLASTQUARTER** function in Power BI DAX returns a table that contains all the dates from the equivalent period in the previous quarter within the same time intelligence level as the input dates. This function is often used for time-based calculations and comparisons when you want to retrieve data from the corresponding period in the previous quarter.

- `<Dates>`: This is the column or table of dates for which you want to find the equivalent period in the previous quarter.

Example:

Suppose you have a financial dataset with a column named "TransactionDate," and you want to calculate the total revenue for the same period (same number of days) in the previous quarter. You can use the **SAMEPERIODLASTQUARTER** function as follows:

DAX Formula:

Total Revenue Last Quarter =
  SUMX(
    FILTER(
      FinancialData,
      NOT(ISBLANK(FinancialData[Revenue]))
    ),
    FinancialData[Revenue]
)

Result: The "Total Revenue Last Quarter" measure will provide the sum of revenue for the equivalent period in the previous quarter.

Tips:

- The **SAMEPERIODLASTQUARTER** function is particularly useful when you need to create quarter-over-quarter comparisons in your Power BI reports.

- Ensure that your date column is marked as a date table within your Power BI data model for this function to work accurately.

- You can adjust the time intelligence level by modifying the `<Dates>` argument. For instance, you can use `[TransactionDate].[Year]` to retrieve the equivalent quarter in the previous year.

- Exercise caution when applying this function in combination with date filters to avoid unexpected results.

The **SAMEPERIODLASTQUARTER** function is a valuable asset for analyzing trends and comparing data between the current and previous quarters, helping you gain insights into your financial or business performance over time.

66.SAMEPERIODLASTYEAR

Syntax:

SAMEPERIODLASTYEAR(<Dates>)

Description:

The **SAMEPERIODLASTYEAR** function in Power BI DAX returns a table that contains all the dates from the equivalent period in the previous year within the same time intelligence level as the input dates. This function is frequently used for time-based calculations and comparisons when you want to retrieve data from the corresponding period in the previous year.

- `<Dates>`: This is the column or table of dates for which you want to find the equivalent period in the previous year.

Example:

Suppose you have a sales dataset with a column named "SalesDate," and you want to calculate the total sales for the same period (same number of days) in the previous year. You can use the **SAMEPERIODLASTYEAR** function as follows:

DAX Formula:

```
Total Sales Last Year =
  SUMX(
    FILTER(
      SalesData,
      NOT(ISBLANK(SalesData[SalesAmount]))
    ),
    SalesData[SalesAmount]
  )
```

Result: The "Total Sales Last Year" measure will provide the sum of sales for the equivalent period in the previous year.

Tips:

- The **SAMEPERIODLASTYEAR** function is particularly useful when you need to create year-over-year comparisons in your Power BI reports.

- Ensure that your date column is marked as a date table within your Power BI data model for this function to work accurately.

- You can adjust the time intelligence level by modifying the `<Dates>` argument. For instance, you can use `[SalesDate].[Quarter]` to retrieve the equivalent quarter in the previous year.

- Be cautious when using this function with date filters, as it can affect the results. Always consider your specific reporting requirements.

The **SAMEPERIODLASTYEAR** function is a valuable tool for analyzing trends and comparing data between the current year and the previous year, helping you gain insights into your sales, performance, or other time-related metrics.

67.SECOND

Syntax:

SECOND(<DateTime>)

Description:

The **SECOND** function in Power BI DAX is used to extract the second component (integer value) from a given date and time.

- `<DateTime>`: This is the date and time column or expression from which you want to extract the second.

Example:

Suppose you have a date and time column named "OrderDateTime," and you want to extract the second component from it. You can use the SECOND function as follows:

DAX Formula:

Order Second = SECOND(Sales[OrderDateTime])

Result: The "Order Second" column will contain the second component (0 to 59) extracted from the "OrderDateTime" column.

Tips:

- The **SECOND** function is particularly useful when you need to perform time-based calculations or create time-based aggregations in your Power BI reports.

- You can use the extracted seconds to create custom time-based calculations, such as calculating the average time spent on a task or analyzing patterns in time-related data.

- Ensure that your "DateTime" column is in the proper datetime format for this function to work accurately.

- You can combine the **SECOND** function with other date and time functions in Power BI to perform more complex calculations, such as calculating the time difference between two datetime values.

The **SECOND** function allows you to work with the second component of datetime values in your Power BI reports, enabling you to analyze and visualize time-related data effectively.

68. TODAY

Syntax:

TODAY()

Description:

The **TODAY** function in Power BI DAX is used to return the current date as a datetime value.

Example:

You can use the **TODAY** function to create a calculated column that displays the current date in a table. Here's an example:

DAX Formula:

Current Date = TODAY()

Result: The "Current Date" column will contain the current date as a datetime value for each row in the table.

Tips:

- The **TODAY** function is particularly useful for creating time-based calculations and tracking data changes over time.

- You can combine the **TODAY** function with other date and time functions in Power BI to perform various date-related calculations, such as calculating the number of days between two dates or determining the day of the week for a given date.

- Keep in mind that the value returned by the **TODAY** function is dynamic and updates automatically every day. Therefore, if you use it in your reports, the date will always reflect the current date when the report is opened or refreshed.

- When using the **TODAY** function, consider formatting the result to display only the date part without the time component, if needed, using formatting functions like **FORMAT** or **DATEVALUE**.

The **TODAY** function allows you to work with the current date in your Power BI reports, making it easier to create time-based calculations and track changes in your data over time.

69. TOTALMTD

Syntax:

TOTALMTD(<expression>, <dates>, [<filter>])

Description:

The **TOTALMTD** function in Power BI DAX is used to calculate the total of an expression year-to-date (YTD) based on the dates provided.

- `<expression>`: This is the expression or measure that you want to calculate year-to-date totals for.

- `<dates>`: This is a column containing the dates for which you want to calculate YTD totals.

- `[<filter>]` (optional): You can specify an optional filter expression to further filter the dates used in the calculation.

Example:

Suppose you have a sales table with a "Date" column and a "SalesAmount" column, and you want to calculate the year-to-date total sales amount for each date.

DAX Formula:

YTD Total Sales = TOTALMTD(SUM(Sales[SalesAmount]), Sales[Date])

Result: The "YTD Total Sales" measure will give you the YTD total of the sales amount for each date in your report.

Tips:

- The **TOTALMTD** function is useful for creating measures that show cumulative totals for a specific expression over time, such as YTD sales, YTD revenue, or YTD expenses.

- You can combine **TOTALMTD** with other time intelligence functions like **DATESYTD** to perform more complex calculations, such as calculating the percentage of total sales for the YTD period.

- Ensure that your date column is correctly marked as a date data type in Power BI for accurate date-based calculations.

- The optional `[<filter>]` parameter allows you to apply additional filters to the date range used for the YTD calculation. This can be useful for scenarios where you want to restrict the calculation to a specific subset of dates.

The **TOTALMTD** function helps you create meaningful year-to-date calculations in your Power BI reports, providing insights into cumulative performance over time.

70. TOTALQTD

Syntax:

TOTALQTD(<expression>, <dates>, [<filter>])

Description:

The **TOTALQTD** function in Power BI DAX is used to calculate the total of an expression quarter-to-date (QTD) based on the dates provided.

- `<expression>`: This is the expression or measure that you want to calculate quarter-to-date totals for.

- `<dates>`: This is a column containing the dates for which you want to calculate QTD totals.

- `[<filter>]` (optional): You can specify an optional filter expression to further filter the dates used in the calculation.

Example:

Suppose you have a sales table with a "Date" column and a "SalesAmount" column, and you want to calculate the quarter-to-date total sales amount for each date.

DAX Formula:

QTD Total Sales = TOTALQTD(SUM(Sales[SalesAmount]), Sales[Date])

Result: The "QTD Total Sales" measure will give you the QTD total of the sales amount for each date in your report.

Tips:

- The **TOTALQTD** function is useful for creating measures that show cumulative totals for a specific expression over a quarter, providing insights into how performance accumulates within a quarter.

- You can combine **TOTALQTD** with other time intelligence functions like **DATESQTD** to perform more complex calculations, such as calculating the percentage of total sales for the QTD period.

- Ensure that your date column is correctly marked as a date data type in Power BI for accurate date-based calculations.

- The optional `[<filter>]` parameter allows you to apply additional filters to the date range used for the QTD calculation. This can be useful for scenarios where you want to restrict the calculation to a specific subset of dates.

The **TOTALQTD** function is a valuable tool for analyzing quarter-to-date data in your Power BI reports, helping you gain insights into cumulative performance within a quarter.

71. TOTALYTD

Syntax:

TOTALYTD(<expression>, <dates>, [<filter>])

Description:

The **TOTALYTD** function in Power BI DAX is used to calculate the total of an expression year-to-date (YTD) based on the dates provided.

- `<expression>`: This is the expression or measure that you want to calculate year-to-date totals for.

- `<dates>`: This is a column containing the dates for which you want to calculate YTD totals.

- `[<filter>]` (optional): You can specify an optional filter expression to further filter the dates used in the calculation.

Example:

Suppose you have a sales table with a "Date" column and a "SalesAmount" column, and you want to calculate the year-to-date total sales amount for each date.

DAX Formula:

YTD Total Sales = TOTALYTD(SUM(Sales[SalesAmount]), Sales[Date])

Result: The "YTD Total Sales" measure will give you the YTD total of the sales amount for each date in your report.

Tips:

- The **TOTALYTD** function is useful for creating measures that show cumulative totals for a specific expression over a year, providing insights into how performance accumulates within a year.

- You can combine **TOTALYTD** with other time intelligence functions like **DATESYTD** to perform more complex calculations, such as calculating the percentage of total sales for the YTD period.

- Ensure that your date column is correctly marked as a date data type in Power BI for accurate date-based calculations.

- The optional `[<filter>]` parameter allows you to apply additional filters to the date range used for the YTD calculation. This can be useful for scenarios where you want to restrict the calculation to a specific subset of dates.

The **TOTALYTD** function is a valuable tool for analyzing year-to-date data in your Power BI reports, helping you gain insights into cumulative performance within a year.

72. YEAR

Syntax:

YEAR(<date>)

Description:

The **YEAR** function in Power BI DAX is used to extract the year component from a given date. It returns an integer representing the year of the provided date.

- `<date>`: This is the date from which you want to extract the year.

Example:

Suppose you have a dataset with a "TransactionDate" column, and you want to create a measure to count the number of transactions that occurred in each year.

DAX Formula:

```
Transactions per Year =
COUNTROWS(
   FILTER(
     TableName,
     YEAR(TableName[TransactionDate]) = 2022
   )
)
```

Result: The "Transactions per Year" measure will count the number of transactions that occurred in the year 2022.

Tips:

- The **YEAR** function is often used in combination with other DAX functions to perform various time-based calculations and aggregations.

- You can use the **YEAR** function to group data by year, create time-based hierarchies, or build custom reports that show trends and patterns over different years.

- Ensure that the column you're using with the **YEAR** function is formatted as a date or date/time data type for accurate results.

- You can also use the **YEAR** function with other DAX functions like **CALCULATE** and **FILTER** to create more complex calculations based on the year component of dates.

The **YEAR** function simplifies date-based calculations in Power BI by allowing you to easily extract and work with the year component of your date data.

CHAPTER VII
Classification Functions

73.ALL

Syntax:

ALL([TableName [, ColumnName] [, ColumnName]...])

Description:

The **ALL** function in Power BI DAX is used to remove filters from one or more columns in a table or from the entire table. It returns a table that includes all the rows from the specified table or columns, while ignoring any context filters that might have been applied.

- `[TableName]`: (Optional) The name of the table from which you want to remove filters. If not specified, it refers to the entire table where the DAX expression is evaluated.

- `[ColumnName]`: (Optional) The name of one or more columns within the specified table from which you want to remove filters.

Example:

Suppose you have a dataset with a "Sales" table containing sales data and a "Products" table containing product information. You want to calculate the total sales for all products regardless of any filters applied to the "Products" table.

DAX Formula:

Total Sales (All Products) =
CALCULATE(
    SUM(Sales[Amount]),
    ALL(Products)
)

Result: The "Total Sales (All Products)" measure will calculate the sum of sales amounts for all products, ignoring any filters applied to the "Products" table.

Tips:

- The **ALL** function is often used in combination with other DAX functions, especially in scenarios where you want to perform calculations with a specific column or table, while disregarding any applied filters.

- You can use the **ALL** function to create more complex measures, such as calculating year-to-date (YTD) or quarter-to-date (QTD) totals, by removing date-related filters.

- When specifying multiple columns within the **ALL** function, it removes filters from all the specified columns, allowing you to focus on a subset of the data while ignoring filters on other columns.

- Be cautious when using the **ALL** function, as it can impact the behavior of other calculations and visualizations in your Power BI report by altering the context in which they operate. Ensure that you use it appropriately based on your reporting requirements.

74. ALLNOBLANKROW

Syntax:

ALLNOBLANKROW([TableName [, ColumnName] [, ColumnName]...])

Description:

The **ALLNOBLANKROW** function in Power BI DAX is used to remove filters from one or more columns in a table or from the entire table, excluding blank rows. It returns a table that includes all the rows from the specified table or columns while ignoring any context filters that might have been applied, but it preserves rows with blank or null values.

- `[TableName]`: (Optional) The name of the table from which you want to remove filters. If not specified, it refers to the entire table where the DAX expression is evaluated.

- `[ColumnName]`: (Optional) The name of one or more columns within the specified table from which you want to remove filters.

Example:

Suppose you have a dataset with a "Sales" table containing sales data and a "Products" table containing product information. You want to calculate the total sales for all products regardless of any filters applied to the "Products" table, but you want to include rows with blank or null product values.

DAX Formula:

Total Sales (All Products, Including Blanks) =

CALCULATE(

   SUM(Sales[Amount]),

   ALLNOBLANKROW(Products)

)

Result: The "Total Sales (All Products, Including Blanks)" measure will calculate the sum of sales amounts for all products, excluding any applied filters on the "Products" table, but preserving rows with blank or null product values.

Tips:

- The **ALLNOBLANKROW** function is especially useful when you want to remove filters but still consider rows with blank or null values in your calculations or visualizations.

- It can be combined with other DAX functions to create complex calculations while ensuring that blank or null values are not removed from the result.

- Carefully consider the use of this function in your reports to avoid unintentional results, as including blank or null values may impact your data analysis and visualization. Use it judiciously based on your specific reporting requirements.

75. ALLSELECTED

Syntax:

ALLSELECTED([TableNameOrColumnName [, TableNameOrColumnName]...])

Description:

The **ALLSELECTED** function in Power BI DAX is used to return a table that includes all the rows from one or more tables or columns, considering the filters and slicers applied in the report visual.

- `[TableNameOrColumnName]`: (Optional) The name of one or more tables or columns from which you want to remove filters. If not specified, it refers to the entire model where the DAX expression is evaluated.

Example:

Suppose you have a report with a "Sales" table and various slicers for filtering data by product category, date, and region. You want to calculate the total sales for all products regardless of the applied slicer selections.

DAX Formula:

Total Sales (All Selected) =

CALCULATE(

   SUM(Sales[Amount]),

ALLSELECTED()

)

Result: The "Total Sales (All Selected)" measure will calculate the sum of sales amounts for all products, considering only the slicer selections made by the user. It removes all other filters and keeps the context set by slicers.

Tips:

- The **ALLSELECTED** function is particularly useful when you want to perform calculations based on the selections made by the report users while preserving the user's context.

- It is commonly used in combination with other DAX functions to create interactive reports and visuals that respond to user selections.

- Be cautious when using **ALLSELECTED** as it can affect the behavior of your measures based on user interactions. Make sure to thoroughly test your reports to ensure they work as expected with different slicer selections.

76. ALLSELECTEDCOLUMNS

Syntax:

ALLSELECTEDCOLUMNS([TableName], [ColumnName], [, [ColumnName]...])

Description:

The **ALLSELECTEDCOLUMNS** function in Power BI DAX is used to return a table that includes selected columns from a specified table, considering the filters and slicers applied in the report visual.

- `[TableName]`: The name of the table from which you want to select columns.

- `[ColumnName]`: One or more names of the columns you want to include in the resulting table.

Example:

Suppose you have a report with a "Sales" table and various slicers for filtering data by product category, date, and region. You want to create a table that includes only the "Product" and "Amount" columns, considering the slicer selections.

DAX Formula:

Filtered Sales =

ALLSELECTEDCOLUMNS(

    Sales,

    "Product",

    "Amount"

)

Result: The "Filtered Sales" table will contain only the "Product" and "Amount" columns from the "Sales" table. It takes into account the slicer selections made by the user, and the resulting table will reflect those selections.

Tips:

- The **ALLSELECTEDCOLUMNS** function is useful when you want to create custom tables based on selected columns from a source table, while considering the user's context through slicer selections.

- You can use the resulting table for further calculations, visualizations, or as a source for other DAX functions and measures.

- Be mindful of the performance impact when using **ALLSELECTEDCOLUMNS**, especially in large datasets. Complex calculations involving many columns may slow down your report's responsiveness.

77.FILTER

Syntax:

FILTER([Table], <FilterExpression>)

Description:

The **FILTER** function in Power BI DAX is used to return a table that includes only the rows that meet a specified condition or criteria. It filters a table based on a Boolean expression provided as the filter condition.

- `[Table]`: The name of the table that you want to filter.

- `<FilterExpression>`: A Boolean expression that specifies the filtering condition. Rows for which the expression evaluates to TRUE are included in the resulting table.

Example:

Suppose you have a "Sales" table with columns like "Product," "Date," and "Revenue." You want to create a table that includes only the rows where the revenue is greater than $1,000.

DAX Formula:

High Revenue Sales =

FILTER(

   Sales,

   Sales[Revenue] > 1000

)

Result: The "High Revenue Sales" table will include only the rows from the "Sales" table where the "Revenue" is greater than $1,000.

Tips:

- The **FILTER** function is commonly used to create custom tables or filter data based on specific criteria. It's a powerful tool for data segmentation and analysis.

- You can use various logical and comparison operators within the filter expression to define complex filtering conditions.

- Be cautious when using the **FILTER** function with large datasets, as it can impact report performance. Consider using it judiciously, especially in complex reports.

78.ISCROSSFILTERED

Syntax:

ISCROSSFILTERED(<Table>)

Description:

The **ISCROSSFILTERED** function in Power BI DAX checks if a specified table has been actively filtered. It returns TRUE if there is an active filter on the specified table; otherwise, it returns FALSE.

- `<Table>`: The name of the table you want to check for active filtering.

Example:

Suppose you have two tables, "Sales" and "Product," and you want to determine if the "Product" table has been actively filtered.

DAX Formula:

Is Product Filtered =

ISCROSSFILTERED('Product')

Result: If the "Product" table has been actively filtered (e.g., by a slicer or a filter), the formula will return TRUE. Otherwise, it will return FALSE.

Tips:

- The **ISCROSSFILTERED** function is useful when you need to conditionally perform calculations or create measures based on whether a specific table is actively filtered.

- You can combine **ISCROSSFILTERED** with other DAX functions to create more complex calculations that respond to user interactions with the report, enhancing the interactivity of your Power BI reports.

- Use this function when you want to create dynamic calculations that adapt to the user's selections and filtering choices.

79.ISSUBTOTAL

Syntax:

ISSUBTOTAL(<Column>)

Description:

The **ISSUBTOTAL** function in Power BI DAX checks if the current row represents a subtotal or grand total in a table or matrix visual. It returns TRUE if the current row is a subtotal or grand total row; otherwise, it returns FALSE.

- `<Column>`: The name of the column you want to check for subtotals or grand totals.

Example:

Suppose you have a table visual that displays sales data, including subtotals and a grand total row. You want to create a measure to identify whether the current row is a subtotal or grand total row.

DAX Formula:

Is Subtotal Row =

ISSUBTOTAL('Sales'[Product])

Result: If the current row in the 'Sales' table represents a subtotal or grand total for the 'Product' column, the formula will return TRUE. Otherwise, it will return FALSE.

Tips:

- The **ISSUBTOTAL** function is commonly used in combination with other DAX functions to create conditional calculations or measures that behave differently for subtotal and grand total rows in visualizations.

- You can use this function to customize the formatting or calculation logic for subtotal and grand total rows, enhancing the clarity and usefulness of your Power BI reports.

- Make sure to specify the appropriate column that corresponds to the subtotals or grand totals you want to detect.

80. TOPN

Syntax:

TOPN(<N>, <Table>, [<Expression>], [<Filter1>], …)

Description:

The **TOPN** function in Power BI DAX is used to retrieve the top N rows from a table based on a specified expression. It is helpful for tasks like identifying the top-performing products or customers.

- `<N>`: An integer that specifies the number of rows to return.

- `<Table>`: The name of the table from which you want to retrieve the top rows.

- `[<Expression>]`: (Optional) An expression that defines the ranking criteria. Rows will be selected based on the values of this expression. If omitted, the function will return the top N rows based on the table's natural order.

- `[<Filter1>]`, `[<Filter2>]`, …: (Optional) Additional filter expressions that you can use to further refine the rows to be considered.

Example:

Suppose you have a 'Sales' table containing data on product sales with columns 'Product', 'Revenue', and 'Quantity.' You want to find the top 5 products based on revenue.

DAX Formula:

Top 5 Products by Revenue =

TOPN(5, 'Sales', 'Sales'[Revenue])

Result: This formula will return a table with the top 5 products based on their revenue.

Tips:

- The **TOPN** function is often used in combination with other DAX functions, such as **FILTER**, to create more complex ranking and filtering logic.

- You can change the direction of ranking (ascending or descending) by using appropriate DAX functions inside the `<Expression>`. For instance, to find the bottom N items, you can use - (minus) to reverse the order.

- Be cautious when using **TOPN** with large datasets, as it can impact performance. Consider using filters and aggregations to optimize your queries.

- For additional control over ranking and filtering, consider using the **RANKX** or **FILTER** functions in conjunction with **TOPN**.

CHAPTER VIII
Statistical Functions

81. AVERAGEA

Syntax:

AVERAGEA(<Column>)

Description:

The **AVERAGEA** function in Power BI DAX is used to calculate the average (arithmetic mean) of all the numbers in a given column, including both numeric and non-numeric values. It treats non-numeric values as zero when performing the calculation.

- `<Column>`: The column or expression containing the values for which you want to calculate the average.

Example:

Suppose you have a 'Sales' table with a 'Revenue' column that includes both numeric values for sales amounts and text values like "Not available." You want to calculate the average revenue, considering all values.

DAX Formula:

Average Revenue = AVERAGEA('Sales'[Revenue])

Result: This formula will calculate the average of all the values in the 'Revenue' column, treating non-numeric values as zero.

Tips:

- **AVERAGEA** is useful when you have a column with mixed data types, and you want to calculate an average while considering all values.

- Be cautious when using **AVERAGEA** with columns that contain text or other non-numeric data. Ensure that the non-numeric values are appropriate for the calculation you intend to perform.

- If you want to calculate the average of only numeric values in a column and ignore non-numeric values, consider using the **AVERAGE** function instead.

- To handle potential errors or divide-by-zero situations, you can combine **AVERAGEA** with error-handling functions like **IFERROR** or **DIVIDE**.

82.CORRELATE

Syntax:

CORRELATE(<Table>, <Columns>, <Table>, <Columns>)

Description:

The **CORRELATE** function in Power BI DAX is used to calculate the correlation coefficient between two tables based on the specified columns. The correlation coefficient measures the strength and direction of a linear relationship between two sets of data. It helps determine if changes in one variable are associated with changes in another variable.

- `<Table>`: The first table for which you want to calculate the correlation coefficient.

- `<Columns>`: The columns from the first table that you want to use for the correlation calculation.

- `<Table>`: The second table for which you want to calculate the correlation coefficient.

- `<Columns>`: The columns from the second table that you want to use for the correlation calculation.

Example:

Suppose you have two tables: 'Sales' and 'Marketing,' and you want to calculate the correlation between the 'Revenue' column in the 'Sales' table and the 'Marketing Spend' column in the 'Marketing' table.

DAX Formula:

Correlation Coefficient = CORRELATE('Sales', 'Revenue', 'Marketing', 'Marketing Spend')

Result: This formula will calculate the correlation coefficient between the two columns, indicating the strength and direction of the relationship between revenue and marketing spend. The result will be a value between -1 and 1, where 1 represents a perfect positive correlation, -1 represents a perfect negative correlation, and 0 represents no correlation.

Tips:

- Use the **CORRELATE** function when you want to quantify the relationship between two sets of data in different tables.

- Ensure that the columns you use for correlation contain numeric data.

- Interpreting the correlation coefficient:

  - A positive coefficient (close to 1) suggests a strong positive linear relationship.

  - A negative coefficient (close to -1) suggests a strong negative linear relationship.

  - A coefficient close to 0 suggests little to no linear relationship.

- Keep in mind that correlation does not imply causation. A high correlation does not necessarily mean one variable causes changes in the other; it only indicates an association.

- The **CORRELATE** function is useful for identifying potential relationships between different aspects of your data, such as sales and marketing spend, temperature and ice cream sales, or customer age and purchase frequency.

83.COVARX.P

Syntax:

COVARX.P(<table>, <column_x>, <column_y>)

Description:

The COVARX.P function in Power BI DAX calculates the population covariance between two columns of data within a specified table. Covariance is a measure that indicates the degree to which two sets of data vary together. It helps to understand whether changes in one variable are associated with changes in another variable.

- `<table>`: The table containing the data you want to use for covariance calculation.

- `<column_x>`: The first column for which you want to calculate covariance.

- `<column_y>`: The second column for which you want to calculate covariance.

Example:

Suppose you have a table called 'Sales' with columns 'Units Sold' and 'Revenue.' You want to calculate the population covariance between these two columns.

DAX Formula:

Population Covariance = COVARX.P('Sales', 'Units Sold', 'Revenue')

Result: This formula will compute the population covariance between 'Units Sold' and 'Revenue' columns in the 'Sales' table.

Tips:

- Use the **COVARX.P** function when you want to measure the degree to which two variables tend to move together within a population.

- The result of the **COVARX.P** function is expressed in the units of the product of the original two columns. It can be positive (indicating that the variables tend to increase or decrease together), negative (indicating that one tends to increase when the other decreases), or close to zero (indicating little to no linear relationship).

- The population covariance is used when you have data for an entire population. If you have data for a sample, you might want to use the **COVAR.P** function, which calculates the sample covariance.

- Remember that covariance does not provide information about the strength or direction of the relationship between variables. It only measures the degree to which they co-vary.

- A positive covariance suggests a tendency for the two variables to move in the same direction, while a negative covariance suggests a tendency for them to move in opposite directions. However, the magnitude of covariance is not easily interpretable by itself.

84.GEOMEAN

Syntax:

GEOMEAN(<table>, <expression>)

Description:

The **GEOMEAN** function in Power BI DAX calculates the geometric mean of a column of values within a specified table. The geometric mean is a statistical measure that represents the average rate of change in a set of values.

- `<table>`: The table containing the data from which you want to calculate the geometric mean.

- `<expression>`: The column or expression for which you want to calculate the geometric mean.

Example:

Suppose you have a table called 'StockReturns' with a column 'DailyReturns' that contains daily percentage returns of a stock. You want to calculate the geometric mean of these daily returns.

DAX Formula:

Geometric Mean = GEOMEAN('StockReturns', 'DailyReturns')

Result: This formula will compute the geometric mean of the 'DailyReturns' column in the 'StockReturns' table.

Tips:

- The geometric mean is particularly useful when dealing with percentages or growth rates because it accounts for the compounding effect. For example, when calculating the average annual growth rate of an investment, the geometric mean is more appropriate than the arithmetic mean.

- The geometric mean is calculated by multiplying all the values together and then taking the nth root, where n is the number of values. In other words, it calculates the central tendency of a set of values by considering their product rather than their sum.

- The **GEOMEAN** function is useful for scenarios where you want to find the average rate of change over a series of values. It is commonly used in finance, biology, and other fields to calculate compound growth rates or averages of ratios.

- Be cautious when using the geometric mean with datasets that contain zero or negative values, as it may not be suitable for such data. In such cases, you may want to filter or clean your data before applying the function.

- The result of the geometric mean is typically expressed as a percentage, representing the average rate of change over the given values.

85. HARMEAN

Syntax:

HARMEAN(<table>, <expression>)

Description:

The **HARMEAN** function in Power BI DAX calculates the harmonic mean of a column of values within a specified table. The harmonic mean is a statistical measure that is used to find the average of rates or ratios.

- `<table>`: The table containing the data from which you want to calculate the harmonic mean.

- `<expression>`: The column or expression for which you want to calculate the harmonic mean.

Example:

Suppose you have a table called 'Speeds' with a column 'Speed' that contains various speed values (e.g., speeds of different vehicles). You want to calculate the harmonic mean of these speed values.

DAX Formula:

Harmonic Mean = HARMEAN('Speeds', 'Speed')

Result: This formula will compute the harmonic mean of the 'Speed' column in the 'Speeds' table.

Tips:

- The harmonic mean is especially useful when dealing with rates or ratios. It provides a more accurate measure of central tendency when the data contains values that vary greatly in magnitude.

- The harmonic mean is calculated by taking the reciprocal of the arithmetic mean of the reciprocals of the values. Mathematically, it is represented as `n / (1/x1 + 1/x2 + ... + 1/xn)`, where n is the number of values, and x1, x2, ..., xn are the individual values.

- Use the harmonic mean when you want to calculate the average of rates or ratios, such as speed, fuel efficiency, or time taken to complete a task.

- Be cautious when using the harmonic mean with datasets that contain zero values because it will result in division by zero. Ensure that your data is appropriate for this calculation.

- The harmonic mean tends to be lower than the arithmetic mean and the geometric mean, especially when there are outliers or extreme values in the dataset.

- Consider using the harmonic mean when you want to find a more balanced measure of central tendency for data that follows a reciprocal relationship, such as time-speed relationships in physics or engineering.

86. MEDIAN

Syntax:

MEDIAN(<table>, <expression>)

Description:

The **MEDIAN** function in Power BI DAX calculates the median of a column of values within a specified table. The median is a statistical measure that represents the middle value of a dataset when it's ordered. It's especially useful when dealing with datasets that may contain outliers or when you want to find the middle value that divides the data into two equal halves.

- `<table>`: The table containing the data from which you want to calculate the median.

- `<expression>`: The column or expression for which you want to calculate the median.

Example:

Suppose you have a table called 'Sales' with a column 'Revenue' that contains various revenue values. You want to calculate the median of these revenue values.

DAX Formula:

Median Revenue = MEDIAN('Sales', 'Revenue')

Result: This formula will compute the median of the 'Revenue' column in the 'Sales' table.

Tips:

- The median is a robust measure of central tendency, which means it is less affected by extreme values (outliers) than the mean (average). It gives you a better sense of the typical value in your data.

- Use the median when you want to find the middle value in a dataset or when you want to understand the distribution of data around a central point.

- The median is calculated by first ordering the data from smallest to largest and then finding the middle value. If there is an even number of data points, the median is the average of the two middle values.

- When working with categorical data or non-numeric data, the MEDIAN function can still be used to find the median based on the sort order of the values.

- Be aware that the median may not always be a value that exists in your dataset. It is the value that divides the data into two equal halves.

- Consider using the median in conjunction with other statistical measures like the mean and standard deviation to gain a comprehensive understanding of your data's distribution.

- If you expect your data to contain extreme outliers, you might also consider calculating the median absolute deviation (MAD) as a robust measure of data spread.

87. MEDIANX

Syntax:

MEDIANX(<table>, <expression>)

Description:

The **MEDIANX** function in Power BI DAX calculates the median of a calculated table or expression. It allows you to create a virtual table by applying a filter or criteria to an existing table and then calculate the median of a specific expression within that virtual table. This function is useful when you need to find the median of a subset of data based on specific conditions.

- `<table>`: The table or expression that defines the dataset from which you want to calculate the median.

- `<expression>`: The expression for which you want to calculate the median within the specified table or expression.

Example:

Suppose you have a table named 'Sales' with columns 'Product', 'Revenue', and 'Region'. You want to calculate the median revenue for products sold only in the 'West' region.

DAX Formula:

Median West Region Revenue = MEDIANX(FILTER('Sales', 'Region' = "West"), 'Revenue')

Result: This formula will create a virtual table by filtering the 'Sales' table for rows where the 'Region' is "West" and then calculate the median of the 'Revenue' column within that filtered table.

Tips:

- The MEDIANX function is especially useful when you need to find the median for specific subsets of your data based on certain conditions or filters.

- It allows you to perform more complex calculations compared to the simple MEDIAN function, as it works with calculated tables.

- Be mindful of the filter conditions you apply within the MEDIANX function, as they determine the subset of data used for median calculation.

- When using MEDIANX, you can combine it with other DAX functions and expressions to create more customized measures and analyze your data more effectively.

- Consider using MEDIANX in scenarios where you need to find the median within dynamic or filtered subsets of your data, such as specific time periods, product categories, or geographic regions.

88.PERCENTILEX.INC

Syntax:

PERCENTILEX.INC(<table>, <expression>, <k>)

Description:

The **PERCENTILEX**.INC function in Power BI DAX calculates the k-th percentile of a dataset, which is the value below which a given percentage of data falls. It operates on a specified table or expression and returns the k-th percentile value based on the provided expression.

- `<table>`: The table or expression that defines the dataset from which you want to calculate the percentile.

- `<expression>`: The expression for which you want to calculate the percentile within the specified table or expression.

- `<k>`: A decimal number between 0 and 1, inclusive, representing the desired percentile. For example, 0.5 corresponds to the 50th percentile, which is the median.

Example:

Suppose you have a table named 'Sales' with a column 'Revenue', and you want to calculate the 25th percentile of the revenue.

DAX Formula:

25th Percentile Revenue = PERCENTILEX.INC('Sales', 'Revenue', 0.25)

Result: This formula will calculate the 25th percentile of the 'Revenue' column within the 'Sales' table.

Tips:

- The PERCENTILEX.INC function is useful for finding specific percentiles of your data, such as quartiles (25th, 50th, 75th percentiles) or other custom percentiles.

- Ensure that the value of `<k>` is between 0 and 1; otherwise, the function will return an error.

- You can combine PERCENTILEX.INC with other DAX functions and expressions to create more complex calculations and analyses based on percentiles.

- Percentiles are helpful for understanding data distributions and identifying data points that fall within specific percent ranges.

- Be cautious when interpreting percentiles, as they may not always provide a complete picture of the data distribution, especially in cases of skewed or non-normal data. Consider visualizing your data alongside percentile calculations for better insights.

89.PERCENTRANK.INC

Syntax:

PERCENTRANK.INC(<table>, <expression>, <value>, [<format>])

Description:

The **PERCENTRANK**.INC function in Power BI DAX calculates the rank of a value in a dataset as a percentage of values below it. It determines the relative standing of a value within a dataset, expressed as a decimal between 0 and 1, inclusive. This function can help you understand how a specific value compares to others in the dataset.

- `<table>`: The table or expression that defines the dataset in which you want to calculate the rank.

- `<expression>`: The expression for which you want to find the rank within the specified table or expression.

- `<value>`: The value for which you want to calculate the percentile rank.

- `[<format>]` (optional): An optional parameter that specifies the format for the result. It accepts values 0 (default) or 1. Use 0 for decimal results (e.g., 0.25 for the 25th percentile) or 1 for percentage results (e.g., 25 for the 25th percentile).

Example:

Suppose you have a table named 'Sales' with a column 'Revenue', and you want to find the percentile rank of a specific revenue value, say $5,000.

DAX Formula:

Percentile Rank of $5,000 = PERCENTRANK.INC('Sales', 'Revenue', 5000, 1)

Result: This formula will calculate the percentile rank of $5,000 in the 'Revenue' column within the 'Sales' table and return it as a percentage. For example, if the result is 0.75, it means that $5,000 is at the 75th percentile, indicating that 75% of the data points have values lower than $5,000.

Tips:

- The PERCENTRANK.INC function is useful for assessing how a specific data point compares to others in the dataset in terms of its position.

- The optional `[<format>]` parameter allows you to control whether the result is presented as a decimal or a percentage.

- Be cautious when interpreting percentile ranks, as they may not provide insights into the distribution shape or outliers in the data. Visualizing data alongside percentile rank calculations can enhance your understanding.

- Consider using PERCENTRANK.INC in combination with other DAX functions to perform more complex analyses or identify values within specific percentile ranges.

90.QUARTILE.INC

Syntax:

QUARTILE.INC(<table>, <expression>, <quartile>)

Description:

The **QUARTILE.INC** function in Power BI DAX calculates the quartile value of a dataset. Quartiles divide a dataset into four equal parts, and this function allows you to find the value that corresponds to a specific quartile.

- `<table>`: The table or expression that defines the dataset for which you want to calculate the quartile.

- `<expression>`: The expression or column for which you want to calculate the quartile.

- `<quartile>`: An integer (1, 2, 3, or 4) representing the quartile you want to calculate. Quartile 1 (Q1) corresponds to the 25th percentile, Quartile 2 (Q2) to the 50th percentile (median), Quartile 3 (Q3) to the 75th percentile, and Quartile 4 (Q4) to the maximum value.

Example:

Suppose you have a table named 'Scores' with a column 'TestScore', and you want to calculate the 25th percentile (Quartile 1) of test scores.

DAX Formula:

Q1 Score = QUARTILE.INC('Scores', 'TestScore', 1)

Result: This formula will calculate the 25th percentile (Quartile 1) of test scores in the 'TestScore' column within the 'Scores' table.

Tips:

- Use the QUARTILE.INC function when you want to analyze the distribution of your data by dividing it into quartiles. Quartiles help you understand the spread and central tendency of your dataset.

- Quartile 1 (Q1) represents the lower 25% of the data, Quartile 2 (Q2) is the median (50th percentile), Quartile 3 (Q3) represents the lower 75%, and Quartile 4 (Q4) represents the maximum value.

- Combine QUARTILE.INC with other DAX functions to perform more complex analyses or identify values within specific quartile ranges.

- Quartiles are useful for identifying potential outliers and assessing the overall variability of your data.

91. RAND

Syntax:

RAND()

Description:

The **RAND** function in Power BI DAX generates a pseudo-random decimal number between 0 and 1. It is commonly used to create random samples or to introduce randomness into your DAX calculations.

- There are no arguments for this function; you simply call it with empty parentheses.

Example:

1. Simple Random Number:

Random Number = RAND()

Result: This formula generates a random decimal number between 0 and 1 each time it's calculated.

Tips:

- The RAND function can be used in various scenarios where randomness is required, such as creating random samples, simulating data, or adding variability to calculations.

- When you refresh your Power BI report, the RAND function recalculates, providing a new random number. This behavior is useful for scenarios where you want to generate different random values upon each refresh.

- To create random integers within a specific range, you can use additional DAX functions such as INT or ROUND in combination with RAND.

- When working with very large datasets, keep in mind that the RAND function can generate a lot of unique random values, so use it judiciously to avoid excessive memory consumption.

92.SMALL

Syntax:

SMALL(<table>, <k>)

Description:

The **SMALL** function in Power BI DAX returns the k-th smallest value from a column in a table. You specify the table and the value of k as arguments. It's a useful function for finding specific data points, such as the second smallest, third smallest, and so on, within a dataset.

- `<table>`: A table or an expression that results in a table.

- `<k>`: The rank of the value you want to find, where 1 represents the smallest value, 2 represents the second smallest, and so on.

Example:

Suppose you have a Sales table with the following data:

Sales Amount
100
150
75
200
125

You can use the SMALL function to find the second smallest sales amount as follows:

Second Smallest Sales = SMALL('Sales', 2)

Result: The Second Smallest Sales measure will return the value 100 because it's the second smallest sales amount in the table.

Tips:

- Ensure that the value of k is a positive integer. If k is less than 1, the SMALL function will return an error.

- If there are duplicate values in the column, the SMALL function will return the k-th smallest unique value. If you need to handle duplicates differently, consider using other functions like MINX in combination with FILTER.

- The SMALL function is useful for various analytical tasks, such as finding percentiles, identifying top or bottom performers, and ranking data points within a dataset.

- Combine the SMALL function with other DAX functions and measures to create more complex calculations and insights in your Power BI reports.

93.STDEV.P

Syntax:

STDEV.P(<column>)

Description:

The **STDEV.P** function in Power BI DAX is used to calculate the standard deviation of a given numeric column within a table. It returns the population standard deviation, which is a measure of the amount of variation or dispersion in a dataset. A lower standard deviation indicates that the values tend to be close to the mean, while a higher standard deviation indicates greater variability.

- `<column>`: The column for which you want to calculate the population standard deviation.

Example:

Suppose you have a Sales table with the following data:

| Sales Amount |

```
|-------------|
| 100      |
| 150      |
| 75       |
| 200      |
| 125      |
```

You can use the STDEV.P function to calculate the population standard deviation of the Sales Amount column as follows:

Population Standard Deviation = STDEV.P('Sales'[Sales Amount])

Result: The Population Standard Deviation measure will return the standard deviation for the given data, which is approximately 45.92 in this case.

Tips:

- Use the STDEV.P function when you want to calculate the standard deviation for an entire population dataset. If you are working with a sample dataset, consider using the STDEV.S function, which calculates the sample standard deviation.

- Standard deviation is a useful statistical measure for understanding the spread of data points. A lower standard deviation indicates that data points are closer to the mean, while a higher standard deviation indicates more variability.

- Combine the STDEV.P function with other DAX functions to perform more advanced statistical analyses in Power BI, such as calculating confidence intervals or identifying outliers in your data.

- Ensure that the column you provide as an argument contains numeric values. Non-numeric or empty values in the column will be ignored in the calculation.

- You can use measures and calculated columns in Power BI to create reusable standard deviation calculations for various parts of your reports and dashboards.

94. VAR

Syntax:

VAR <variable_name> = <expression>

RETURN <variable_name>

Description:

The **VAR** function in Power BI DAX is used for defining and assigning values to variables within a DAX formula. It allows you to store intermediate results or calculations, making your DAX code more readable and efficient. The **VAR** function is typically used within other DAX functions or calculations to simplify complex expressions.

- `<variable_name>`: A user-defined name for the variable.

- `<expression>`: The calculation or expression that you want to assign to the variable.

The result of the **VAR** function is the value assigned to the variable, which can then be used in subsequent calculations within the same DAX formula.

Example:

Suppose you want to calculate the total sales for a specific region while also displaying the total sales for all regions. You can use the **VAR** function to define a variable to hold the total sales for the selected region, like this:

Total Sales =

VAR SelectedRegion = "North"

RETURN

  CALCULATE(

    SUM('Sales'[Sales Amount]),

    'Sales'[Region] = SelectedRegion

)

In this example:

- `SelectedRegion` is a variable that holds the value "North."

- The `Total Sales` measure calculates the sum of sales amount for the selected region using the `CALCULATE` function.

Tips:

- Use the **VAR** function to improve the readability and maintainability of your DAX code, especially for complex calculations or when you need to reuse intermediate results multiple times within a formula.

- Variables in DAX are local to the formula in which they are defined. They cannot be used in other measures or calculations.

- Be cautious with variable names to avoid conflicts with column or table names in your data model.

- Variables can be useful when dealing with complex filter contexts or scenarios where you want to calculate something based on a condition.

- The **VAR** function is an essential tool for optimizing DAX code. By breaking down complex calculations into smaller, more manageable pieces, you can improve the performance of your Power BI reports and dashboards.

95. VAR.P

Syntax:

VAR.P(<expression>)

Description:

The **VAR.P** function in Power BI DAX is used to calculate the variance of a population dataset. It calculates the average of the squared differences between each data point and the population mean. This function is useful for statistical analysis when you have access to the entire population data and want to understand the variability within that population.

- `<expression>`: A DAX expression that represents the dataset for which you want to calculate the variance.

The result of the **VAR.P** function is a numeric value representing the variance of the population dataset.

Example:

Suppose you have a dataset of exam scores for all students in a school, and you want to calculate the population variance of these scores. You can use the **VAR.P** function as follows:

Population Variance =

VAR.P('Exam Scores'[Score])

In this example:

- `'Exam Scores'[Score]` represents the dataset of exam scores for the entire population.

- The `Population Variance` measure calculates the population variance using the **VAR.P** function.

Result: The `Population Variance` measure will display the population variance of the exam scores dataset.

Tips:

- Use the **VAR.P** function when you have data for the entire population and want to measure the variability within that population.

- Population variance is a valuable statistic for understanding the spread or dispersion of data points in a population.

- Be cautious when interpreting the variance value, as it is in squared units of the original data. To get a better sense of data dispersion, consider taking the square root of the variance to calculate the standard deviation (use the SQRT function).

- Make sure to use appropriate data modeling and filtering techniques to ensure that you are working with the entire population when using the VAR.P function.

- The **VAR.P** function can be combined with other statistical functions to perform more in-depth analyses in Power BI.

96. VARIANCE.P

Syntax:

VARIANCE.P(<expression>)

Description:

The **VARIANCE.P** function in Power BI DAX is used to calculate the sample variance of a dataset. It calculates the average of the squared differences between each data point and the sample mean. This function is useful for statistical analysis when you have a sample dataset and want to estimate the variability within that sample.

- `<expression>`: A DAX expression that represents the dataset for which you want to calculate the sample variance.

The result of the **VARIANCE.P** function is a numeric value representing the sample variance of the dataset.

Example:

Suppose you have a dataset of exam scores for a sample of students, and you want to calculate the sample variance of these scores. You can use the **VARIANCE.P** function as follows:

Sample Variance =

VARIANCE.P('Sample Exam Scores'[Score])

In this example:

- ``Sample Exam Scores'[Score]` represents the dataset of exam scores for the sample of students.

- The `Sample Variance` measure calculates the sample variance using the VARIANCE.P function.

Result: The `Sample Variance` measure will display the sample variance of the exam scores dataset.

Tips:

- Use the **VARIANCE.P** function when you have a sample dataset and want to estimate the variability within that sample.

- Sample variance is a valuable statistic for understanding the spread or dispersion of data points in a sample.

- Be cautious when interpreting the variance value, as it is in squared units of the original data. To get a better sense of data dispersion, consider taking the square root of the variance to calculate the sample standard deviation (use the **SQRT** function).

- Ensure that your dataset accurately represents the sample you are interested in, and that it is appropriately filtered and aggregated before using the **VARIANCE.P** function.

- The **VARIANCE.P** function can be combined with other statistical functions to perform more in-depth analyses in Power BI.

CHAPTER IX
Calculation Functions

97.AVERAGEX

Syntax:

AVERAGEX(<table>, <expression>)

Description:

The **AVERAGEX** function in Power BI DAX is used to calculate the average (arithmetic mean) of a numeric expression over a table. It iterates through the rows of the specified table, evaluates the expression for each row, and then computes the average of those expression results.

- `<table>`: The table over which you want to iterate to calculate the average.

- `<expression>`: A DAX expression that represents the numeric values for which you want to calculate the average.

The result of the **AVERAGEX** function is a numeric value representing the average of the expression evaluated for each row in the table.

Example:

Suppose you have a table called `Sales` with columns `Product` and `Revenue`, and you want to calculate the average revenue per product. You can use the **AVERAGEX** function as follows:

Average Revenue per Product =

AVERAGEX(Sales, Sales[Revenuc])

In this example:

- `Sales` is the table over which you want to iterate.

- `Sales[Revenue]` is the numeric expression representing the revenue for each product.

- The `Average Revenue per Product` measure calculates the average revenue using the **AVERAGEX** function.

Result: The `Average Revenue per Product` measure will display the average revenue per product.

Tips:

- Use the **AVERAGEX** function when you want to calculate the average of a numeric expression over a table.

- This function is useful for aggregating data and finding averages based on specific criteria or conditions.

- Ensure that the `<expression>` you provide results in a numeric value for each row in the `<table>`. If not, you may get unexpected results.

- You can combine the **AVERAGEX** function with other DAX functions to perform more complex calculations and analysis.

- Be mindful of the context in which you use the **AVERAGEX** function, as it can be affected by filters, row-level security, and relationships between tables.

98.COUNTX

Syntax:

COUNTX(<table>, <expression>)

Description:

The **COUNTX** function in Power BI DAX is used to count the number of rows in a table that meet a specified condition, determined by the provided expression. It iterates through the rows of the specified table, evaluates the expression for each row, and counts the rows for which the expression evaluates to a non-blank result.

- `<table>`: The table over which you want to iterate and count rows.

- `<expression>`: A DAX expression that represents the condition to be met for counting rows.

The result of the **COUNTX** function is an integer representing the count of rows that meet the specified condition.

Example:

Suppose you have a table called `Orders` with columns `OrderID` and `OrderAmount`, and you want to count the number of orders with an amount greater than $100. You can use the **COUNTX** function as follows:

High-Value Orders Count =

COUNTX(Orders, IF(Orders[OrderAmount] > 100, 1, BLANK()))

In this example:

- `Orders` is the table over which you want to iterate.

- `IF(Orders[OrderAmount] > 100, 1, BLANK())` is the expression that checks if the `OrderAmount` is greater than $100 for each row. If true, it returns `1`; otherwise, it returns a blank value.

- The `High-Value Orders Count` measure calculates the count of rows meeting the condition using the **COUNTX** function.

Result: The `High-Value Orders Count` measure will display the count of orders with amounts greater than $100.

Tips:

- Use the **COUNTX** function when you need to count rows in a table based on a specified condition.

- Ensure that the `<expression>` provided results in a numeric value for each row in the `<table>`. It should return `1` for rows that meet the condition and `BLANK()` for rows that don't.

- The **COUNTX** function can be combined with other DAX functions and used in more complex calculations and measures.

- Be aware of the context in which you use the **COUNTX** function, as it can be influenced by filters, relationships, and row-level security settings.

- When the condition is met, **COUNTX** counts both non-blank values and explicit `0` values in the result.

99.CROSSFILTER

Syntax:

CROSSFILTER(<table>, <table>, <crossfilterType>)

Description:

The **CROSSFILTER** function in Power BI DAX is used to specify the type of filtering to be applied when filtering data between two tables in a data model. It defines how filters should propagate from one table (the source) to another table (the target). This function is primarily used when working with bidirectional filtering in relationships between tables.

- `<table>` (Source Table): The table from which filtering originates.

- `<table>` (Target Table): The table to which filtering is applied.

- `<crossfilterType>`: An integer that represents the type of cross-filtering to be used. It accepts the following values:

  - `0` (None): No cross-filtering is applied. Filters do not propagate from the source table to the target table.

  - `1` (Single): Single-directional cross-filtering is applied. Filters propagate from the source table to the target table.

  - `2` (Both): Bidirectional cross-filtering is applied. Filters propagate from the source table to the target table and vice versa.

Example:

Suppose you have two tables, `Sales` and `Products`, with a relationship between them based on the `ProductID` column. By default, this relationship applies single-directional filtering, meaning filters in the `Sales` table affect the `Products` table but not the other way around. To change this to bidirectional filtering, you can use the **CROSSFILTER** function:

CALCULATE(SUM(Sales[SalesAmount]), CROSSFILTER(Products, Sales, Both))

In this example:

- `Products` is the source table.

- `Sales` is the target table.

- `Both` is used as the `<crossfilterType>` to enable bidirectional cross-filtering.

- The measure calculates the sum of sales amounts but considers bidirectional cross-filtering between the two tables.

Result: The measure will produce results considering both source-to-target and target-to-source filtering based on the bidirectional filter setting.

Tips:

- Use the **CROSSFILTER** function when you need to control the direction of filtering between tables, especially when bidirectional filtering is required.

- Bidirectional filtering can impact performance and query results, so use it judiciously based on your specific modeling requirements.

- Be cautious when enabling bidirectional filtering as it may lead to unexpected results or performance issues in complex models. Test thoroughly before implementing it in a production environment.

- Understand the relationships between tables in your data model to determine when and where to use the **CROSSFILTER** function effectively.

- Properly documenting the use of bidirectional filtering is essential for maintaining and troubleshooting complex Power BI models.

100. DIVIDE

Syntax:

DIVIDE(<numerator>, <denominator>, <alternativeResult>)

Description:

The **DIVIDE** function in Power BI DAX is used to perform division operations. It calculates the result of dividing the `<numerator>` by the `<denominator>`. If the `<denominator>` is zero, it can return an alternative result, which is helpful to avoid division by zero errors.

- `<numerator>`: The value that you want to divide. It's the dividend in the division operation.

- `<denominator>`: The value by which you want to divide. It's the divisor in the division operation.

- `<alternativeResult>` (optional): The value to return if the `<denominator>` is zero. If omitted, the function will return a blank value if division by zero occurs.

Example:

Suppose you have a table with sales data, and you want to calculate the sales margin percentage, which is the sales profit divided by the total sales amount. You can use the DIVIDE function to handle cases where there's no profit (division by zero):

Sales Margin % = DIVIDE([Sales Profit], [Total Sales Amount], 0)

In this example:

- `[Sales Profit]` is the numerator.

- `[Total Sales Amount]` is the denominator.

- `0` is specified as the `<alternativeResult>` in case the denominator is zero.

Result: The measure calculates the sales margin percentage, handling division by zero gracefully and returning 0% when there's no profit.

Tips:

- Use the **DIVIDE** function when you need to perform division operations and want to handle division by zero scenarios gracefully.

- Specifying an `<alternativeResult>` helps avoid errors and ensures that your calculations provide meaningful results, even when dividing by zero.

- Be cautious when using the **DIVIDE** function, as it may return unexpected results if not used correctly. Always validate your calculations and test edge cases.

- You can format the result of the **DIVIDE** function as a percentage in Power BI visuals for a more user-friendly display.

- When designing reports and dashboards, consider using the **DIVIDE** function to create meaningful KPIs and metrics that involve ratios or percentages.

101. MAXX

Syntax:

MAXX(<table>, <expression>)

Description:

The **MAXX** function in Power BI DAX is used to calculate the maximum value of an expression for each row in a specified table. It iterates through the rows of the table, evaluates the expression for each row, and returns the maximum value found.

- `<table>`: The table over which you want to iterate to find the maximum value.

- `<expression>`: The expression to be evaluated for each row in the table, and the maximum of these values is returned.

Example:

Suppose you have a table named "Sales" with columns "Product" and "Revenue," and you want to find the maximum revenue for each product category. You can use the **MAXX** function as follows:

Max Revenue per Category =

MAXX(

SUMMARIZE(Sales, Sales[Product], "Total Revenue", SUM(Sales[Revenue])),

[Total Revenue]

)

In this example:

- `SUMMARIZE` is used to create a summary table that groups sales by product and calculates the total revenue for each product.

- `[Total Revenue]` is the expression to find the maximum of the total revenue for each product category.

Result: The measure returns the maximum revenue value for each product category.

Tips:

- Use the **MAXX** function when you need to find the maximum value of an expression for each row in a table.

- The **MAXX** function is often used in combination with other DAX functions like `SUMMARIZE` to create more complex calculations.

- Be mindful of performance when using **MAXX** with large tables, as it involves iterating through the entire table.

- Consider using other statistical functions like **MAX** or **MAXA** for simpler cases where you need to find the maximum value without row-level calculations.

- Always ensure that the `<expression>` used in **MAXX** makes sense in the context of your analysis and provides meaningful results.

102. MINX

Syntax:

MINX(<table>, <expression>)

Description:

The **MINX** function in Power BI DAX is used to calculate the minimum value of an expression for each row in a specified table. It iterates through the rows of the table, evaluates the expression for each row, and returns the minimum value found.

- `<table>`: The table over which you want to iterate to find the minimum value.

- `<expression>`: The expression to be evaluated for each row in the table, and the minimum of these values is returned.

Example:

Suppose you have a table named "Sales" with columns "Product" and "Revenue," and you want to find the minimum revenue for each product category. You can use the **MINX** function as follows:

Min Revenue per Category =

MINX(

    SUMMARIZE(Sales, Sales[Product], "Total Revenue", SUM(Sales[Revenue])),

[Total Revenue]

)

In this example:

- `SUMMARIZE` is used to create a summary table that groups sales by product and calculates the total revenue for each product.

- `[Total Revenue]` is the expression to find the minimum of the total revenue for each product category.

Result: The measure returns the minimum revenue value for each product category.

Tips:

- Use the **MINX** function when you need to find the minimum value of an expression for each row in a table.

- The **MINX** function is often used in combination with other DAX functions like `SUMMARIZE` to create more complex calculations.

- Be mindful of performance when using **MINX** with large tables, as it involves iterating through the entire table.

- Consider using other statistical functions like **MIN** or **MINA** for simpler cases where you need to find the minimum value without row-level calculations.

- Always ensure that the `<expression>` used in **MINX** makes sense in the context of your analysis and provides meaningful results.

103. SELECTEDVALUE

Syntax:

SELECTEDVALUE(<column>)

Description:

The **SELECTEDVALUE** function in Power BI DAX is used to retrieve the single value from a specified column when there is only one distinct value selected in a filter context. It is commonly used when you expect a single selection, such as from a slicer, and want to capture that selected value for calculations or display.

- `<column>`: The column from which you want to retrieve the selected value.

Example:

Suppose you have a slicer for selecting a product category, and you want to display the selected category name. You can use the **SELECTEDVALUE** function as follows:

Selected Category = SELECTEDVALUE(Products[Category])

In this example:

- `Products[Category]` is the column from which you want to retrieve the selected value.

- If a single product category is selected in the slicer, this measure will return that category's name. If multiple categories are selected, or no category is selected, it will return a blank value.

Result: The measure returns the selected product category when only one category is chosen; otherwise, it returns blank.

Tips:

- Use the **SELECTEDVALUE** function when you want to capture a single selected value from a column in a filter context.

- Be cautious when using **SELECTEDVALUE** as it assumes that only one value is selected. If multiple values are selected, it will return a blank.

- You can provide a second argument to the **SELECTEDVALUE** function, which serves as the default value to return if no or multiple values are selected. For example: `SELECTEDVALUE(Products[Category], "Multiple Categories Selected")`.

- Ensure that the column you're using with **SELECTEDVALUE** contains unique values or that your business logic guarantees a single selection.

104. SUMMARIZE

Syntax:

SUMMARIZE(<table>, <grouping_column(s)>, [<name/value pairs>])

Description:

The **SUMMARIZE** function in Power BI DAX is used to create a summary table that aggregates data from a specified table. It allows you to group data by one or more columns and calculate aggregations or expressions for each group. This function is particularly useful for generating summary reports or creating new tables based on specific criteria.

- `<table>`: The table from which you want to create a summary.

- `<grouping_column(s)>`: One or more columns by which you want to group the data. You can specify multiple columns to create a multi-level grouping.

- `[<name/value pairs>]`: An optional list of name/value pairs that defines additional columns in the resulting summary table. These columns can contain calculated expressions or aggregations based on the grouped data.

Example:

Suppose you have a sales dataset with columns like "Product," "Region," "Date," and "Sales Amount." You want to create a summary table that shows the total sales amount for each product in each region. You can use the **SUMMARIZE** function as follows:

Sales Summary =

SUMMARIZE(

    Sales,

    Products[Product],

    Geography[Region],

    "Total Sales", SUM(Sales[Sales Amount])

)

In this example:

- `Sales` is the source table.

- `Products[Product]` and `Geography[Region]` are the grouping columns.

- "Total Sales" is an alias for the calculated column that sums the "Sales Amount" for each group.

Result: The **SUMMARIZE** function creates a summary table with columns "Product," "Region," and "Total Sales" containing the grouped data.

Tips:

- **SUMMARIZE** is commonly used to create summary tables for reporting or visualization purposes.

- You can include multiple grouping columns to create a multi-level summary.

- The name/value pairs allow you to create calculated columns within the summary table, which can be useful for aggregations or expressions.

- Be mindful of performance when using **SUMMARIZE**, especially with large datasets. It can be resource-intensive for complex summaries.

- You can further filter the summarized table using other DAX functions or by adding additional filtering conditions.

105. SUMMARIZEC

Syntax:

SUMMARIZEC(<table>, <grouping_column(s)>, [<filter_table>])

Description:

The **SUMMARIZEC** function in Power BI DAX is used to create a summarized table with specified groupings and an optional filter table. It is similar to the **SUMMARIZE** function but allows you to apply additional filters to the summarized table.

- `<table>`: The table from which you want to create a summary.

- `<grouping_column(s)>`: One or more columns by which you want to group the data.

- `[<filter_table>]`: An optional table that can be used to filter the summarized table based on conditions defined in the filter table.

Example:

Suppose you have a sales dataset with columns like "Product," "Region," "Date," and "Sales Amount." You want to create a summary table that shows the total sales amount for each product in each region but filtered by a specific region. You can use the **SUMMARIZEC** function as follows:

Filtered Sales Summary =

SUMMARIZEC(

   Sales,

   Products[Product],

   FILTER('Geography', 'Geography'[Region] = "North"),

   "Total Sales", SUM(Sales[Sales Amount])

)

In this example:

- `Sales` is the source table.

- `Products[Product]` is the grouping column.

- `FILTER('Geography', 'Geography'[Region] = "North")` filters the summarized table to include only data where the region is "North."

- "Total Sales" is an alias for the calculated column that sums the "Sales Amount" for each group.

Result: The **SUMMARIZEC** function creates a summary table with columns "Product" and "Total Sales" containing the grouped and filtered data.

Tips:

- **SUMMARIZEC** is useful when you want to create a summary table with specific filters applied to it.

- You can include multiple grouping columns to create a multi-level summary.

- Be mindful of performance when using **SUMMARIZEC**, especially with large datasets. It can be resource-intensive for complex summaries.

- The filter table allows you to define filtering conditions based on the columns of the summary table and apply those conditions while summarizing the data.

106. SUMX

Syntax:

SUMX(<table>, <expression>)

Description:

The **SUMX** function in Power BI DAX is used to iterate through a table and calculate the sum of a specified expression for each row of the table. It then returns the total sum of all those individual calculations.

- `<table>`: The table over which you want to iterate to calculate the sum.

- `<expression>`: The expression or measure that you want to sum for each row in the table.

Example:

Suppose you have a sales dataset with columns like "Product," "Quantity," and "Price," and you want to calculate the total sales amount. You can use the **SUMX** function as follows:

Total Sales =

SUMX(Sales, Sales[Quantity] * Sales[Price])

In this example:

- `Sales` is the table you want to iterate over.

- `Sales[Quantity] * Sales[Price]` is the expression to calculate the sales amount for each row.

Result: The **SUMX** function calculates the sales amount for each row and returns the total sum of those individual sales amounts.

Tips:

- **SUMX** is particularly useful when you need to perform calculations row by row within a table and then aggregate those results.

- You can use **SUMX** to create custom measures that involve complex calculations for each row.

- Be cautious with the performance of **SUMX** when dealing with large datasets, as it may iterate over a significant number of rows, which can impact query performance.

- Ensure that the expression you provide to **SUMX** returns a numeric value, as it is a summation function.

CHAPTER X
Aggregation Functions

107. AVERAGE

Syntax:

AVERAGE(<expression>)

Description:

The **AVERAGE** function in Power BI DAX is used to calculate the arithmetic mean of a numeric expression over a table of data. It adds up all the values in the specified column or expression and divides the sum by the count of non-blank values to find the average.

- `<expression>`: The column or expression containing the numeric values for which you want to calculate the average.

Example:

Suppose you have a sales dataset with a "SalesAmount" column, and you want to calculate the average sales amount:

Average Sales = AVERAGE(Sales[SalesAmount])

In this example:

- `Sales[SalesAmount]` is the column that contains the numeric values (sales amounts).

Result: The **AVERAGE** function adds up all the sales amounts in the specified column and divides the sum by the count of non-blank values in that column to calculate the average sales amount.

Tips:

- Use the **AVERAGE** function when you need to find the central tendency or typical value of a set of numeric data.

- Ensure that the column or expression provided to the **AVERAGE** function contains numeric values; otherwise, it will return unexpected results.

- The **AVERAGE** function automatically handles blank or null values and does not include them in the calculation.

- You can use the **AVERAGE** function in combination with other DAX functions to create more complex calculations and measures in Power BI.

108. COUNT

Syntax:

COUNT(<expression>)

Description:

The **COUNT** function in Power BI DAX is used to count the number of rows in a table or the number of values in a column or expression. It returns the count of all rows in a table or the count of non-blank values in a column or expression.

- `<expression>`: The column or expression for which you want to count rows or values.

Example:

Suppose you have a sales dataset with a "SalesAmount" column, and you want to count the number of sales transactions:

Count Sales Transactions = COUNT(Sales[SalesAmount])

In this example:

- `Sales[SalesAmount]` is the column containing the values you want to count, which are sales transactions.

Result: The **COUNT** function counts the number of non-blank values in the specified column, giving you the count of sales transactions.

Tips:

- Use the **COUNT** function when you want to know the number of rows in a table or the number of non-blank values in a column.

- The **COUNT** function counts only non-blank values. Blank or null values are not included in the count.

- You can use the **COUNT** function with other DAX functions to perform more complex calculations and create measures in Power BI.

- To count all rows in a table, use the **COUNTROWS** function. Use **COUNT** when you specifically want to count non-blank values in a column or expression.

109. COUNTA

Syntax:

COUNTA(<expression>)

Description:

The **COUNTA** function in Power BI DAX is used to count the number of non-blank values in a column or expression. It returns the count of all non-blank values within the specified column or expression.

- `<expression>`: The column or expression for which you want to count non-blank values.

Example:

Suppose you have a product dataset with a "Product Name" column, and you want to count the number of non-blank product names:

Count Non-Blank Product Names = COUNTA(Product[Product Name])

In this example:

- `Product[Product Name]` is the column containing the values you want to count, which are product names.

Result: The **COUNTA** function counts the number of non-blank values in the specified column, giving you the count of non-blank product names.

Tips:

- Use the **COUNTA** function when you want to count non-blank values in a column or expression.

- Unlike the **COUNT** function, which counts only non-blank numeric values, **COUNTA** counts all non-blank values, including text, numbers, logical values, and errors.

- Blank or null values are not included in the count.

- You can use the **COUNTA** function with other DAX functions to perform more complex calculations and create measures in Power BI.

110. COUNTAX

Syntax:

COUNTAX(<table>, <expression>)

Description:

The COUNTAX function in Power BI DAX is used to count the number of rows in a table that meet a specified condition based on a given expression. It returns the count of rows where the expression evaluates to a non-blank value.

- `<table>`: The table or table expression you want to count rows from.

- `<expression>`: The expression that defines the condition. Rows for which this expression returns a non-blank result will be counted.

Example:

Suppose you have a sales dataset with a "Sales" table, and you want to count the number of sales transactions where the sales amount is greater than $1,000:

Count High-Value Sales = COUNTAX(Sales, IF(Sales[Amount] > 1000, 1, BLANK()))

In this example:

- `Sales` is the table containing the sales data.

- `Sales[Amount] > 1000` is the condition that checks if the sales amount is greater than $1,000.

- The **COUNTAX** function counts the rows in the "Sales" table where the expression evaluates to a non-blank value (1 if the condition is met, otherwise BLANK()).

Result: The **COUNTAX** function returns the count of sales transactions with amounts greater than $1,000.

Tips:

- Use the **COUNTAX** function when you want to count rows based on a specific condition or expression.

- The expression can be more complex and include logical and mathematical operations.

- Rows that evaluate to a blank result in the expression are not included in the count.

- You can use the **COUNTAX** function in measures and calculated columns to create custom calculations in Power BI.

111. DISTINCTCOUNT

Syntax:

DISTINCTCOUNT(<column>)

Description:

The **DISTINCTCOUNT** function in Power BI DAX is used to count the number of unique, distinct values in a column. It returns the count of unique items in the specified column.

- `<column>`: The column or column expression for which you want to count distinct values.

Example:

Let's say you have a sales dataset with a "Product" table, and you want to count the number of unique products sold:

Unique Product Count = DISTINCTCOUNT(Product[Product Name])

In this example:

- `Product[Product Name]` is the column from which you want to count distinct values, which is the product names.

- The **DISTINCTCOUNT** function counts the number of unique product names in the "Product" table.

Result: The **DISTINCTCOUNT** function returns the count of unique products sold.

Tips:

- Use the **DISTINCTCOUNT** function when you need to count the number of distinct or unique values in a column.

- It is commonly used for creating measures that involve counting unique items, such as counting unique customers, products, or categories.

- The function helps in performing analytics where deduplicating data or counting unique occurrences is essential.

- You can use it in combination with other DAX functions to create more complex measures and calculations in Power BI.

112. MAX

Syntax:

MAX(<column>)

Description:

The **MAX** function in Power BI DAX is used to find the maximum (largest) value within a specified column. It returns the highest value from the column.

- `<column>`: The column or column expression from which you want to find the maximum value.

Example:

Suppose you have a "Sales" table with a "Revenue" column, and you want to find the maximum revenue:

Max Revenue = MAX(Sales[Revenue])

In this example:

- `Sales[Revenue]` is the column from which you want to find the maximum value, which represents revenue.

- The **MAX** function calculates and returns the highest revenue value in the "Sales" table.

Result: The **MAX** function returns the maximum revenue value in the "Sales" table.

Tips:

- Use the **MAX** function when you need to find the largest value within a column, such as maximum sales, highest temperature, or maximum order quantity.

- You can use this function to create calculated measures or columns that capture the maximum value for specific attributes in your dataset.

- The function is often used in combination with other DAX functions to create more complex calculations and metrics in Power BI.

- Be cautious when using **MAX** with text columns, as it returns the text value that is lexicographically highest (not numerically highest).

- To find the minimum (smallest) value, you can use the **MIN** function, which is the counterpart of **MAX**.

113. ROLLUP

Syntax:

ROLLUP(<table>, <column_name>, [<grouping_column>])

Description:

The **ROLLUP** function in Power BI DAX is used for aggregating data hierarchically. It generates subtotals and grand totals for a given column, allowing you to analyze data at different levels of granularity. This function is particularly useful when working with hierarchies, such as time-based hierarchies (e.g., year, quarter, month, day).

- `<table>`: The name of the table that contains the data you want to aggregate.

- `<column_name>`: The name of the column for which you want to create subtotals and grand totals.

- `[<grouping_column>]` (optional): A column that represents the hierarchy or grouping levels. If specified, it generates subtotals and grand totals for each unique value in this column.

Example:

Suppose you have a "Sales" table with the columns "Year," "Quarter," and "Revenue." You want to calculate subtotals and grand totals for revenue at both the year and quarter levels. Here's how you can use the **ROLLUP** function:

Total Revenue by Year and Quarter =

ROLLUP('Sales', 'Sales'[Revenue], 'Sales'[Year], 'Sales'[Quarter])

In this example:

- `'Sales'` is the name of the table.

- `'Sales'[Revenue]` is the column for which you want to calculate subtotals and grand totals.

- `'Sales'[Year]` and `'Sales'[Quarter]` represent the hierarchy levels. The function generates subtotals and grand totals for each unique combination of year and quarter.

Result: The **ROLLUP** function returns a table with subtotals and grand totals for the specified hierarchy levels.

Tips:

- Use the **ROLLUP** function when you want to create hierarchical aggregations in your data model, such as subtotals for different levels of a time-based hierarchy.

- You can use this function in combination with other DAX functions to perform calculations on aggregated data effectively.

- Be mindful of the hierarchy levels you specify, as generating subtotals and grand totals for too many levels can lead to a large result set, impacting performance.

- This function is particularly useful in scenarios where you need to drill down or roll up data within a hierarchy in visuals like PivotTables and matrices.

- The **ROLLUP** function is similar to the **CUBEVALUE** function in Excel, allowing you to work with hierarchical data in a similar way.

114. MIN

Syntax:

MIN(<column>)

Description:

The **MIN** function in Power BI DAX is used to find the minimum (smallest) value within a specified column. It returns the lowest value from the column.

- `<column>`: The column or column expression from which you want to find the minimum value.

Example:

Suppose you have a "Sales" table with a "Quantity" column, and you want to find the minimum quantity sold:

Min Quantity = MIN(Sales[Quantity])

In this example:

- `Sales[Quantity]` is the column from which you want to find the minimum value, representing the quantity sold.

- The **MIN** function calculates and returns the lowest quantity value in the "Sales" table.

Result: The **MIN** function returns the minimum quantity sold in the "Sales" table.

Tips:

- Use the **MIN** function when you need to find the smallest value within a column, such as the minimum quantity, lowest temperature, or minimum order amount.

- You can use this function to create calculated measures or columns that capture the minimum value for specific attributes in your dataset.

- The function is often used in combination with other DAX functions to create more complex calculations and metrics in Power BI.

- Be cautious when using **MIN** with text columns, as it returns the text value that is lexicographically lowest (not numerically lowest).

- To find the maximum (largest) value, you can use the **MAX** function, which is the counterpart of **MIN**.

115. ROLLUPADDISSUBTOTAL

Syntax:

ROLLUPADDISSUBTOTAL(<table>, <column_name>, <expression>, <new_row_name>, [<grouping_column>])

Description:

The **ROLLUPADDISSUBTOTAL** function in Power BI DAX is used to enhance the functionality of the **ROLLUP** function. It calculates subtotals and grand totals for a specified column, but it also allows you to add custom subtotal rows to the result table, typically for special calculations or additional context.

- `<table>`: The name of the table that contains the data you want to aggregate.

- `<column_name>`: The name of the column for which you want to create subtotals and grand totals.

- `<expression>`: An expression that calculates a custom subtotal or grand total. This expression is evaluated for each subtotal row.

- `<new_row_name>`: A string that represents the name of the custom subtotal row that will be added to the result table.

- `[<grouping_column>]` (optional): A column that represents the hierarchy or grouping levels. If specified, it generates subtotals and grand totals for each unique value in this column.

Example:

Suppose you have a "Sales" table with the columns "Year," "Quarter," "Month," and "Revenue." You want to calculate subtotals and grand totals for revenue at the year, quarter, and month levels. Additionally, you want to add a custom subtotal row that calculates the average revenue for each year. Here's how you can use the **ROLLUPADDISSUBTOTAL** function:

Total Revenue by Year, Quarter, and Month =

ROLLUPADDISSUBTOTAL(

    'Sales',

    'Sales'[Revenue],

    AVERAGE('Sales'[Revenue]),

    "Average Revenue per Year",

    'Sales'[Year],

    'Sales'[Quarter],

    'Sales'[Month]

)

In this example:

- `'Sales'` is the name of the table.

- `'Sales'[Revenue]` is the column for which you want to calculate subtotals and grand totals.

- `AVERAGE('Sales'[Revenue])` is the expression that calculates the average revenue for each year.

- `"Average Revenue per Year"` is the name of the custom subtotal row.

- `'Sales'[Year]`, `'Sales'[Quarter]`, and `'Sales'[Month]` represent the hierarchy levels for which subtotals and grand totals are calculated.

Result: The **ROLLUPADDISSUBTOTAL** function returns a table with subtotals, grand totals, and the custom subtotal row for the specified hierarchy levels.

Tips:

- Use the **ROLLUPADDISSUBTOTAL** function when you want to calculate subtotals and grand totals along with custom subtotal rows for additional context or special calculations.

- The custom subtotal row is particularly useful when you need to display additional summary information in your report or visualization.

- Be cautious when adding custom subtotals, as they can increase the complexity of your data model and visuals. Only add them when they provide valuable insights.

- Ensure that the expression used to calculate custom subtotals aligns with your analysis requirements and provides meaningful information to your audience.

CHAPTER XI
String Handling Functions

116. BLANK

Syntax:

BLANK()

Description:

The **BLANK** function in Power BI DAX is a simple function that returns a blank (null) value. It is often used to represent missing or empty values in calculations, and it can be helpful for handling missing data in your data model.

- `BLANK()`: This function does not require any arguments and simply returns a blank value.

Example:

Let's say you have a sales dataset with missing values in the "Quantity" column, and you want to calculate the total sales. You can use the BLANK function to handle these missing values gracefully:

Total Sales = SUMX('Sales', 'Sales'[Price] * IF(ISBLANK('Sales'[Quantity]), BLANK(), 'Sales'[Quantity]))

In this example:

- ``Sales`` is the name of the table.

- ``Sales'[Price]` represents the price of each item.

- ``Sales'[Quantity]` is the column with potentially missing values.

The formula calculates the total sales by multiplying the price by the quantity, but it uses the **BLANK** function to return a blank value if the quantity is missing for any row.

Result: The "Total Sales" measure handles missing quantity values without affecting the calculation.

Tips:

- Use the **BLANK** function when you want to handle missing or empty values in your calculations or expressions.

- BLANK values are different from zeros or empty strings, and they are typically treated as unknown or missing data points.

- When working with BLANK values, be aware of how they might affect your calculations and visualizations. You can use functions like **IF** and **ISBLANK** to conditionally handle BLANK values based on your specific requirements.

- BLANK values can be useful for avoiding errors and ensuring that your calculations and reports provide accurate insights, even when dealing with incomplete data.

117. BLANKROW

Syntax:

BLANKROW(table)

Description:

The **BLANKROW** function in Power BI DAX is used to create a blank row within a table. This blank row can be used for various purposes, such as creating placeholder rows for future data, generating a blank row for specific calculations, or performing outer joins with other tables.

- `table`: This is the table for which you want to create a blank row.

Example:

Suppose you have a table named "Sales" with columns "Product" and "Quantity," and you want to create a blank row to represent an empty sale. You can use the BLANKROW function as follows:

Blank Sale = BLANKROW('Sales')

In this example, "Sales" is the name of the table, and the `Blank Sale` measure creates a blank row with the same column structure as the "Sales" table.

Result: The "Blank Sale" measure produces a table with a single blank row, where both the "Product" and "Quantity" columns have null values.

Tips:

- The **BLANKROW** function is useful when you need to generate blank rows in a table for various purposes, such as data modeling, calculations, or creating relationships with other tables.

- You can use this function in combination with other DAX functions to perform operations that require a blank row as a placeholder.

- When creating relationships between tables, a blank row can be used to represent a scenario where there is no match between tables.

- Be cautious when using blank rows in calculations, as they can affect the behavior of certain functions and aggregations. Ensure that your calculations handle blank rows appropriately based on your specific requirements.

118. CONCATENATEX

Syntax:

CONCATENATEX(table, delimiter, expression, [order_by], [filter])

Description:

The **CONCATENATEX** function in Power BI DAX is used to concatenate values from a column within a table into a single text string, separated by a specified delimiter. This function is especially useful when you want to aggregate and display a list of values as a comma-separated string, for example, to summarize related data.

- `table`: The table containing the data you want to concatenate.

- `delimiter`: The text or character that separates the concatenated values in the resulting string.

- `expression`: The expression or column containing the values you want to concatenate.

- `[order_by]` (optional): An expression or column by which to sort the values before concatenation.

- `[filter]` (optional): An optional filter expression to apply before concatenating the values.

Example:

Suppose you have a table named "Orders" with columns "OrderID" and "Product," and you want to create a concatenated list of products for each order, separated by commas. You can use the **CONCATENATEX** function as follows:

Concatenated Products = CONCATENATEX('Orders', ', ', 'Product', 'OrderID')

In this example:

- `'Orders'` is the name of the table.

- `', '` is the delimiter (a comma and a space) used to separate the concatenated values.

- `'Product'` is the expression that specifies the column containing the values you want to concatenate.

- `'OrderID'` is used for sorting the values by the "OrderID" column.

Result: The "Concatenated Products" measure produces a single text string for each order, with the products concatenated and separated by commas.

Tips:

- The **CONCATENATEX** function is particularly handy for creating summarized text representations of data, such as creating a list of items within a category.

- You can use filtering conditions to control which values are included in the concatenation, allowing you to create dynamic summaries based on specific criteria.

- Be mindful of performance when using this function with large datasets, as concatenating a large number of values can impact report performance.

119. LEFT

Syntax:

LEFT(text, num_chars)

Description:

The **LEFT** function in Power BI DAX is used to extract a specified number of characters from the beginning (left side) of a text string.

- `text`: The text string from which you want to extract characters.

- `num_chars`: The number of characters you want to extract from the beginning of the text.

Example:

Suppose you have a table with a column named "Product Name," and you want to create a new column that contains the first three characters of each product name. You can use the **LEFT** function as follows:

First Three Characters = LEFT('Table'[Product Name], 3)

In this example:

- `'Table'[Product Name]` is the column containing the text strings.

- `3` specifies that you want to extract the first three characters from each text string.

Result: The "First Three Characters" column will contain the first three characters of each product name.

Tips:

- The **LEFT** function is useful when you need to extract a specific portion of text from a longer string.

- You can combine the **LEFT** function with other text manipulation functions or columns to create more complex expressions.

- Be cautious when specifying the number of characters to extract; if it exceeds the length of the text string, it will return the entire string.

120. LOWER

Syntax:

LOWER(text)

Description:

The **LOWER** function in Power BI DAX is used to convert all characters in a text string to lowercase. It is a useful function for standardizing text data, making it case-insensitive for comparisons or display purposes.

- `text`: The text string you want to convert to lowercase.

Example:

Let's say you have a table with a column named "Customer Name," and you want to create a new column that contains all customer names in lowercase. You can use the LOWER function as follows:

Lowercase Name = LOWER('Table'[Customer Name])

In this example:

- `'Table'[Customer Name]` is the column containing the customer names.

Result: The "Lowercase Name" column will contain all the customer names converted to lowercase.

Tips:

- The **LOWER** function is helpful when you need to perform case-insensitive searches or comparisons on text data.

- You can use this function in combination with other text manipulation or analysis functions to achieve specific tasks.

- Keep in mind that the **LOWER** function only converts text to lowercase; it does not affect numbers or non-alphabetical characters in the text.

121. MID

may be more MID Function in Power BI DAX

Syntax:

MID(text, start_num, num_chars)

Description:

The **MID** function in Power BI DAX is used to extract a substring from a text string. It returns a specified number of characters from the middle of a text string, starting at a specified position.

- `text`: The text string from which you want to extract a substring.

- `start_num`: The position in the text string from which to start extracting characters. The first character is at position 1.

- `num_chars`: The number of characters to extract from the text string.

Example:

Suppose you have a table with a column named "Product Name," and you want to create a new column that extracts the middle three characters from each product name, starting from the second character. You can use the **MID** function as follows:

Mid Extract = MID('Table'[Product Name], 2, 3)

In this example:

- `'Table'[Product Name]` is the column containing the product names.

- `2` specifies that extraction should start from the second character.

- `3` specifies that three characters should be extracted.

Result: The "Mid Extract" column will contain the extracted substrings.

Tips:

- The **MID** function is useful for parsing text data and extracting specific portions of text.

- Be cautious when using the `start_num` and `num_chars` arguments to ensure you don't exceed the length of the text string, which could result in errors.

- You can combine the **MID** function with other text functions for more complex text manipulation tasks.

- The **MID** function is case-sensitive, so it distinguishes between uppercase and lowercase letters in the text string.

122. PATHCONTAINS

Syntax:

PATHCONTAINS(path, value)

Description:

The **PATHCONTAINS** function in Power BI DAX is used to determine if a given path or hierarchy contains a specific value. It checks whether the specified value exists in the hierarchy, and if so, it returns TRUE; otherwise, it returns FALSE.

- `path`: The path or hierarchy to be checked for the presence of the value.

- `value`: The value to be checked for existence within the specified path or hierarchy.

Example:

Suppose you have a table that represents a product hierarchy with a column named "Product Path," and you want to create a calculated column that checks if a specific product, "ProductXYZ," exists within the hierarchy. You can use the **PATHCONTAINS** function as follows:

Product Exists = PATHCONTAINS('Table'[Product Path], "ProductXYZ")

In this example:

- `'Table'[Product Path]` is the column containing the product hierarchy path.

- `"ProductXYZ"` is the value you want to check for.

Result: The "Product Exists" column will contain TRUE if "ProductXYZ" exists in the hierarchy specified in the "Product Path" column, and FALSE if it does not.

Tips:

- The **PATHCONTAINS** function is particularly useful when dealing with hierarchical data structures, such as product categories, organizational hierarchies, or folder structures.

- Make sure that the path or hierarchy you provide is correctly formatted and matches the structure of your data. If the hierarchy is not correctly defined, the function may not return the expected results.

- You can use the result of the **PATHCONTAINS** function in conditional expressions or to filter data based on the existence of a specific value within a hierarchy.

- This function is often used in combination with other DAX functions to perform more complex calculations and filtering operations within hierarchies.

123. PATHITEM

Syntax:

PATHITEM(path, index)

Description:

The **PATHITEM** function in Power BI DAX is used to retrieve a specific item from a hierarchy or path. It allows you to extract an element from a path based on its position within the hierarchy.

- `path`: The path or hierarchy from which you want to extract an item.

- `index`: The position of the item you want to retrieve from the hierarchy. The index starts at 1 for the first item in the hierarchy.

Example:

Suppose you have a table that represents a product hierarchy with a column named "Product Path," and you want to create a calculated column that extracts the third-level product category from the hierarchy. You can use the **PATHITEM** function as follows:

Category = PATHITEM('Table'[Product Path], 3)

In this example:

- `'Table'[Product Path]` is the column containing the product hierarchy path.

- `3` is the index of the third-level category you want to extract.

Result: The "Category" column will contain the name of the third-level product category for each row.

Tips:

- The **PATHITEM** function is particularly useful when working with hierarchical data structures, such as product categories, organizational hierarchies, or folder structures, and you need to extract specific elements from those hierarchies.

- Ensure that the index you provide is within the valid range of the hierarchy. If the index is out of range, the function will return a blank value.

- You can use the result of the **PATHITEM** function in various calculations or to create summary reports based on specific hierarchy levels.

- This function can be combined with other DAX functions to perform more complex operations on hierarchical data, such as aggregations or filtering based on specific hierarchy levels.

124. PATHITEMREVERSE

Syntax:

PATHITEMREVERSE(path, index)

Description:

The **PATHITEMREVERSE** function in Power BI DAX is used to retrieve a specific item from a hierarchy or path in reverse order. It allows you to extract an element from a path based on its position within the hierarchy, starting from the end.

- `path`: The path or hierarchy from which you want to extract an item.

- `index`: The position of the item you want to retrieve from the hierarchy in reverse order. The index starts at 1 for the last item in the hierarchy.

Example:

Suppose you have a table that represents a file system hierarchy with a column named "File Path," and you want to create a calculated column that extracts the name of the parent folder (the second-to-last item) from the hierarchy. You can use the **PATHITEMREVERSE** function as follows:

ParentFolder = PATHITEMREVERSE('Table'[File Path], 2)

In this example:

- `'Table'[File Path]` is the column containing the file system hierarchy path.

- `2` is the index of the second-to-last item (the parent folder) you want to extract.

Result: The "ParentFolder" column will contain the name of the parent folder for each file path.

Tips:

- The **PATHITEMREVERSE** function is particularly useful when working with hierarchical data structures, such as file system paths or URLs, and you need to extract elements from the hierarchy in reverse order.

- Ensure that the index you provide is within the valid range of the hierarchy. If the index is out of range, the function will return a blank value.

- You can use the result of the **PATHITEMREVERSE** function in various calculations or to create summary reports based on specific hierarchy levels in reverse order.

- This function can be combined with other DAX functions to perform more complex operations on hierarchical data, such as aggregations or filtering based on specific hierarchy levels in reverse order.

125. PATHLENGTH

Syntax:

PATHLENGTH(path)

Description:

The **PATHLENGTH** function in Power BI DAX is used to calculate the length or depth of a hierarchy or path. It returns the number of elements or levels in a given hierarchy.

- `path`: The hierarchy or path for which you want to calculate the length.

Example:

Suppose you have a table that represents a file system hierarchy with a column named "File Path," and you want to create a calculated column that calculates the depth or length of each file path. You can use the **PATHLENGTH** function as follows:

PathDepth = PATHLENGTH('Table'[File Path])

In this example:

- `'Table'[File Path]` is the column containing the file system hierarchy path.

Result: The "**PathDepth**" column will contain the depth or length of each file path, indicating the number of levels in the hierarchy.

Tips:

- The **PATHLENGTH** function is valuable when working with hierarchical data structures, such as file system paths or organizational hierarchies, and you need to understand the depth of each element.

- The result of this function can be used for various purposes, such as identifying the depth of a specific item in a hierarchy, aggregating data at different hierarchy levels, or creating conditional logic based on hierarchy depth.

- Ensure that the provided path is well-structured, and elements within the hierarchy are properly delimited, as the function relies on the structure of the path to determine the length.

- This function is useful in combination with other DAX functions to perform complex calculations or to filter and aggregate data at specific hierarchy depths.

126. PATHLENGTHREVERSE

Syntax:

PATHLENGTHREVERSE(path)

Description:

The **PATHLENGTHREVERSE** function in Power BI DAX is used to calculate the length or depth of a hierarchy or path in reverse order. It returns the number of elements or levels in a given hierarchy when counted from the bottom (leaf) to the top (root).

- `path`: The hierarchy or path for which you want to calculate the reverse length.

Example:

Suppose you have a table that represents a file system hierarchy with a column named "File Path," and you want to create a calculated column that calculates the depth or length of each file path in reverse order. You can use the PATHLENGTHREVERSE function as follows:

ReversePathDepth = PATHLENGTHREVERSE('Table'[File Path])

In this example:

- `'Table'[File Path]` is the column containing the file system hierarchy path.

Result: The "ReversePathDepth" column will contain the reverse depth or length of each file path, indicating the number of levels in the hierarchy when counted from the leaf to the root.

Tips:

- The **PATHLENGTHREVERSE** function is valuable when working with hierarchical data structures and you need to understand the depth of each element when counted in reverse order.

- This function is particularly useful when dealing with hierarchies where you want to identify how deep each element is from the bottom (leaf) of the hierarchy to the top (root).

- Ensure that the provided path is well-structured, and elements within the hierarchy are properly delimited, as the function relies on the structure of the path to determine the reverse length.

- You can use the result of this function for various purposes, such as identifying the depth of a specific item from the bottom of the hierarchy, aggregating data from the leaf to the root, or creating conditional logic based on reverse hierarchy depth.

- Consider combining this function with other DAX functions to perform complex calculations or to filter and aggregate data at specific hierarchy depths in reverse order.

127. PROPER

Syntax:

PROPER(text)

Description:

The **PROPER** function in Power BI DAX is used to capitalize the first letter of each word in a text string and convert all other letters to lowercase. It is particularly useful when you want to standardize the capitalization of text, making it more visually appealing.

- `text`: The text string that you want to convert to title case.

Example:

Suppose you have a column named "Product Name" in your table, and you want to create a new column that displays the product names in title case (capitalizing the first letter of each word). You can use the **PROPER** function as follows:

TitleCaseProductName = PROPER('Table'[Product Name])

In this example:

- `'Table'[Product Name]` is the column containing the product names.

Result: The "TitleCaseProductName" column will contain the product names with the first letter of each word capitalized and all other letters in lowercase.

Tips:

- The **PROPER** function is helpful for ensuring consistent and standardized text formatting, especially when dealing with text data from various sources or when displaying data to end-users.

- You can use this function in calculated columns to transform text data for better readability and presentation.

- Keep in mind that the **PROPER** function does not change the original text in the source column; it creates a new column with the properly formatted text.

- If you need to modify the original column in place, you can use Power Query's Text Transformations or other text manipulation functions.

- Be cautious when using the **PROPER** function with data that contains acronyms or specific terms that should remain in uppercase. You may need to combine it with other functions or apply exceptions to preserve the desired capitalization for certain words or phrases.

128. RIGHT

Syntax:

RIGHT(text, num_chars)

Description:

The **RIGHT** function in Power BI DAX is used to extract a specified number of characters from the end (right side) of a text string. It helps you retrieve a portion of a text string starting from the last character and moving towards the first character.

- `text`: The text string from which you want to extract characters.

- `num_chars`: The number of characters you want to extract from the right end of the text string.

Example:

Suppose you have a column named "Order Number" in your table, and you want to create a new column that contains the last three characters of each order number. You can use the RIGHT function as follows:

LastThreeChars = RIGHT('Table'[Order Number], 3)

In this example:

- `'Table'[Order Number]` is the column containing the order numbers.

- `3` is the number of characters to extract from the right end.

Result: The "LastThreeChars" column will contain the last three characters of each order number.

Tips:

- The **RIGHT** function is helpful for extracting specific portions of text from the end of a string, such as the last few characters of product codes, order numbers, or file extensions.

- You can use negative values for `num_chars` to extract characters from the end of the text string, counting backward. For example, `RIGHT("Hello, World", -5)` would return "World" because it starts from the 5th character from the right.

- Be cautious when specifying `num_chars` to ensure that it doesn't exceed the length of the text string, as doing so will result in an empty string.

- If you're dealing with variable-length text strings and want to ensure that you always get a certain number of characters from the end, you can use functions like **LEN** to calculate the length of the text string dynamically.

- The **RIGHT** function can be used in calculated columns or measures depending on your specific use case for text manipulation in Power BI.

129. SUBSTITUTE

Syntax:

SUBSTITUTE(text, old_text, new_text, [occurrence])

Description:

The **SUBSTITUTE** function in Power BI DAX is used to replace occurrences of a specified old text within a text string with new text. It allows you to perform a search-and-replace operation on a given text.

- `text`: The text string where you want to replace occurrences of `old_text` with `new_text`.

- `old_text`: The text you want to find and replace.

- `new_text`: The text you want to replace `old_text` with.

- `[occurrence]` (optional): An optional parameter that specifies which occurrence of `old_text` to replace. If not provided, all occurrences are replaced.

Example:

Suppose you have a column named "Product Description," and you want to replace all occurrences of "old" with "new" within that column. You can use the **SUBSTITUTE** function as follows:

Updated Description = SUBSTITUTE('Table'[Product Description], "old", "new")

In this example:

- `'Table'[Product Description]` is the column containing the product descriptions.

- `"old"` is the text you want to find and replace.

- `"new"` is the text you want to replace "old" with.

Result: The "Updated Description" column will contain the product descriptions with all occurrences of "old" replaced by "new."

Tips:

- The **SUBSTITUTE** function is useful for cleaning and transforming text data by replacing specific terms, characters, or patterns.

- If you want to replace only a specific occurrence of `old_text`, you can use the `[occurrence]` parameter to control which instance is replaced. For example, `SUBSTITUTE("abc abc abc", "abc", "XYZ", 2)` would replace the second occurrence of "abc" with "XYZ."

- To replace all occurrences of `old_text`, simply omit the `[occurrence]` parameter or provide a large number, such as `999`, to ensure all instances are replaced.

- The **SUBSTITUTE** function is case-sensitive, meaning it treats "old" and "Old" as different text. If you want a case-insensitive search and replace, you can use the **REPLACE** function in combination with other DAX functions to achieve the desired result.

- Be cautious when replacing text, as it may affect the integrity of your data. Always review and verify the results to ensure they meet your expectations.

130. TRIM

Syntax:

TRIM(text)

Description:

The **TRIM** function in Power BI DAX is used to remove extra spaces (leading and trailing spaces) from a text string. It helps clean up text data by eliminating unnecessary whitespace characters.

- `text`: The text string from which you want to remove extra spaces.

Example:

Suppose you have a column named "Customer Names," and some of the names have extra spaces at the beginning and end. You can use the **TRIM** function to clean up the data as follows:

Cleaned Names = TRIM('Table'[Customer Names])

In this example:

- `'Table'[Customer Names]` is the column containing customer names.

Result: The "Cleaned Names" column will contain the customer names with extra spaces removed.

Tips:

- The **TRIM** function is particularly useful when working with data that may have been imported from external sources or user inputs, as it ensures that leading and trailing spaces don't interfere with your analysis.

- Keep in mind that **TRIM** only removes leading and trailing spaces. It does not remove extra spaces between words within the text.

- If you need to remove both leading/trailing spaces and extra spaces between words, you can use a combination of functions. For example, you can use **TRIM** followed by the **SUBSTITUTE** function to replace multiple spaces with a single space.

- While **TRIM** is commonly used for cleaning up text data, it may not be necessary for all scenarios. Always assess your data and determine if removing extra spaces is essential for your analysis.

131. UNICHAR

Syntax:

UNICHAR(number)

Description:

The **UNICHAR** function in Power BI DAX is used to return the Unicode character that corresponds to a given Unicode number. It allows you to work with characters and symbols that are not available on your keyboard by specifying their Unicode code point.

- `number`: An integer representing the Unicode code point of the character you want to retrieve.

Example:

Let's say you want to display a special Unicode character in your report, such as the "thumbs up" symbol (), which has a Unicode code point of U+1F44D. You can use the UNICHAR function as follows:

Thumbs Up Symbol = UNICHAR(128077)

In this example:

- `128077` is the Unicode code point for the "thumbs up" symbol.

Result: The "Thumbs Up Symbol" measure will display the "▯" symbol in your report.

Tips:

- The **UNICHAR** function is handy when you need to include special characters or symbols in your Power BI reports that are not readily available on your keyboard.

- You can find the Unicode code points for various characters and symbols on Unicode character charts and websites. Simply provide the appropriate Unicode code point as an argument to **UNICHAR** to display the desired character.

- Make sure your report's font supports the character you want to display, as some fonts may not include all Unicode characters. You may need to adjust your report's font settings if the character does not appear correctly.

- Unicode characters can enhance the visual appeal and informativeness of your reports, especially when dealing with international or specialized content.

132. UNICHARACTER

Syntax:

UNICHARACTER(code)

Description:

The **UNICHARACTER** function in Power BI DAX is used to return the Unicode character that corresponds to a given Unicode code point. It is similar to the UNICHAR function, but it takes a text argument instead of a number.

- `code`: A text value representing the Unicode code point of the character you want to retrieve.

Example:

Suppose you want to display the "thumbs up" symbol (□), which has a Unicode code point of U+1F44D. You can use the **UNICHARACTER** function as follows:

Thumbs Up Symbol = UNICHARACTER("U+1F44D")

In this example:

- `"U+1F44D"` is the text representation of the Unicode code point for the "thumbs up" symbol.

Result: The "Thumbs Up Symbol" measure will display the "□" symbol in your report.

Tips:

- The **UNICHARACTER** function is useful when you want to include special characters or symbols in your Power BI reports by specifying the Unicode code point as a text value.

- You can find the Unicode code points for various characters and symbols on Unicode character charts and websites. Simply provide the appropriate Unicode code point as a text argument to **UNICHARACTER** to display the desired character.

- Ensure that your report's font supports the character you want to display, as some fonts may not include all Unicode characters. You may need to adjust your report's font settings if the character does not appear correctly.

- Unicode characters can enhance the visual appeal and informativeness of your reports, especially when dealing with international or specialized content.

133. UPPER

Syntax:

UPPER(text)

Description:

The **UPPER** function in Power BI DAX is used to convert all characters in a text string to uppercase. It takes a text argument and returns a new text string with all characters converted to uppercase.

- `text`: The text or text column you want to convert to uppercase.

Example:

Suppose you have a column named "Product Name" with various product names in mixed case, and you want to convert them all to uppercase for consistency. You can use the UPPER function as follows:

Uppercase Product Name = UPPER('Product Table'[Product Name])

In this example:

- `'Product Table'[Product Name]` is the column containing the product names.

Result: The "Uppercase Product Name" column will display all product names in uppercase.

Tips:

- The **UPPER** function is useful when you want to standardize the case of text data for consistency in your Power BI reports.

- It is a case-insensitive function, meaning that it will convert all characters to uppercase regardless of their current case.

- If you need to convert text to lowercase, you can use the **LOWER** function instead.

- Ensure that the column or text you provide as an argument to **UPPER** contains the text data you want to convert. The function does not modify the original text; it creates a new text string with uppercase characters.

CONCLUSION

Note: The functions introduced here represent a selection of DAX functions in Power BI. There are many more DAX functions available for various purposes, including aggregation, filtering, and calculations. Learning how to use different DAX functions effectively is essential for mastering Power BI and creating powerful data models and reports.

Conclusion:

In this series of introductions to Power BI DAX functions, we've covered a wide range of functions that are commonly used for data manipulation, calculations, and transformations in Power BI. These functions enable you to perform tasks such as filtering data, aggregating values, working with dates and times, and manipulating text.

Power BI's DAX language is a powerful tool for data modeling and analysis, allowing you to create complex calculations and measures that can provide valuable insights into your data. Whether you're a beginner or an experienced Power BI user, understanding how to use DAX functions effectively is crucial for harnessing the full potential of Power BI.

We hope these introductions have been helpful in building your understanding of some key DAX functions. If you want to explore more DAX functions or dive deeper into specific topics, consider further resources, training, or consulting to expand your knowledge.

Thank You: We sincerely thank you for choosing our book and for your interest in learning about Power BI DAX functions. We hope this content has been valuable in your journey to becoming a proficient Power BI user. If you have any questions or need further assistance, please don't hesitate to reach out. Happy data modeling and reporting with Power BI!

Made in United States
North Haven, CT
10 November 2023

43870431R00143